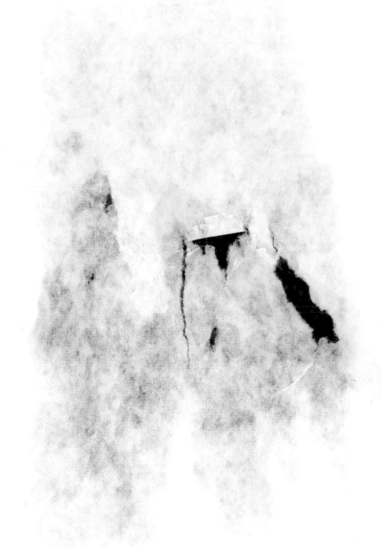

THE EQUAL PAY ACT

THE EQUAL PAY ACT

Implications for Comparable Worth

Walter Fogel

PRAEGER SPECIAL STUDIES • PRAEGER SCIENTIFIC

New York • Philadelphia • Eastbourne, UK
Toronto • Hong Kong • Tokyo • Sydney

Library of Congress Cataloging in Publication Data

Fogel, Walter A.
  The Equal Pay Act.

  Includes indexes.
  1. Equal pay for equal work—Law and legislation—
United States. 2. Sex discrimination against women—
Law and legislation—United States. I. Title.
KF3467.F63 1984   344.73 '0121 84-11594
ISBN 0-03-071789-2 (alk. paper) 347.304121

Published in 1984 by Praeger Publishers
CBS Educational and Professional Publishing
a Division of CBS Inc.
521 Fifth Avenue, New York, NY 10175 USA
© 1984 by Praeger Publishers

56789 052 9876543

Printed in the United States of America
on acid-free paper

ACKNOWLEDGEMENTS

I gratefully acknowledge support for the preparation of this book from the Institute of Industrial Relations, University of California, Los Angeles.

This book is dedicated to my three children, Susan Mary, Peter Antrim, and Cathleen Ann.

Walter Fogel

CONTENTS

LIST OF TABLES

THE EQUAL PAY ACT

1
INTRODUCTION

The text of the Equal Pay Act of 1963 (EPA) is quite brief. Its prohibition of unequal pay for equal work is set forth in 150 words:

> No employer having employees subject to any provisions of this section shall discriminate, within any establishment in which such employees are employed, between employees on the basis of sex by paying wages to employees in such establishment at a rate less than the rate at which he pays employees of the opposite sex in such establishment for equal work on jobs the performance of which requires equal skill, effort, and responsibility, and which are performed under similar working conditions, except where such payment is made pursuant to (i) a seniority system; (ii) a merit system; (iii) a system which measures earnings by quantity or quality of production; or (iv) a differential based on any other factor other than sex: *Provided*, That an employer who is paying a wage rate differential in violation of this subsection shall not, in order to comply with the provisions of this subsection, reduce the wage rate of any employee.[1]

Put into the context that motivated this legislation, these words mean that employers cannot pay women less than they pay men when both are performing equal work on the employer's premises, except when the greater pay to men (or women) is justified by a widely accepted standard such as seniority, merit, or output.

This prohibition, which represents a legislative embodiment of the slogan "equal pay for equal work," is almost universally endorsed as equitable. Yet, there is reason to doubt the need for the prohibition and to doubt that it has accomplished much for the case of female equity since it became law in 1963. These doubts were the impetus for my examination of the EPA and for this book. After some preliminary thinking about the matter, I arrived at certain beliefs that formed the working hypotheses for my study: (1) that the Act would have relatively little application; (2) that its

1

interpretation and application by the courts would be difficult; (3) that some of the court decisions applying the Act would not make economic sense.

1. My belief that the EPA would not have widespread application was based partly on the statute's narrow focus. First, it applies only within a particular business establishment; at most, that concept encompasses a single firm or governmental unit. Equal pay cannot be required for women in firm A who are doing work equal to that of higher paid men in firm B, even if the two firms are immediately adjacent to each other. Second, the law applies only when women are doing work that is *equal* to that of men. Although early decisions ruled that in this context "equal" does not mean "identical" or "the same," they also held that it does mean "substantially the same." Consequently, equal pay for nurses' aides (females) and orderlies (males) in hospitals may be required because, in some instances, their work is substantially equal; however, the law does nothing for nurses who think they should receive the same pay as hospital electricians, for example, because these two jobs cannot be conceived as substantially equal in job content, equal as they may be in the training, skill, effort, and responsibility requirements for performance of the two jobs.

I also saw the EPA as having a limited application because it was likely that, as of 1963, few employers were actually paying unequal wages for equal work. I reasoned that this was because (a) they saw it as poor personnel practice and (b) it did not make good business sense. Employers generally find it a poor personnel practice to pay different wage rates to employees doing the same work within an establishment unless the pay differences are clearly based upon meritorious factors such as seniority or quantity of sales. When meritorious differences are not present, the practice of giving unequal pay risks hostile reactions by the lower paid employees—they see it as unfair. When the unequal pay is systematically based upon sex, it is likely to be perceived as unfair at least by most females. Although pay irrationalities among individuals and groups of workers have been common in industrial history, modern personnel practice views these irrationalities as incompatible with good employee relations.

Unequal pay for equal work makes no business sense because, if employers were able to hire women for a particular job at a lower rate than that required to hire men, why would they hire men at all for the job? Instead, they would hire only women, thereby saving wage costs as well as possible costs from female resentment over unequal wages. As a consequence of employers' desire to pay as little as required by the market to get a job done, men and women will ordinarily not be found within an establishment performing equal work at different hourly or weekly wage rates. One can imagine circumstances where this conclusion does not hold, and these will be discussed in the next chapter, but such circumstances are not common.

2. The idea that the courts would have difficulty in interpreting and applying the EPA was based on my beliefs that (a) because unequal pay for equal work is rare, the language of the statute must be stretched for it to have any significant application; (b) the concept of equal work is difficult to define and apply to the tasks of actual jobs; and (c) wage determination is a murky process that encompasses numerous influences. The implication of the last belief is that wage discrimination is much more difficult to identify and remedy than is job discrimination.

3. Finally, my belief that some of the court decisions applying the EPA would not make economic sense cannot be surprising, because the Act was intended to interfere with market processes and economic calculations that produce low pay for women. That intent may have been somewhat misplaced, because a competitive labor market will produce only one wage for a job that employs both men and women; nonetheless, some EPA court decisions can be expected to favor notions of female equity at the expense of economic efficiency. It is one thing, however, to say that the EPA was intended to interfere with certain economic practices. The question of the economic impacts actually produced still needs examination. Consequently, this question formed one of the bases for my investigations.

These initial critical bases for my interest in the EPA did not mean that I thought the law should never have been passed. Even if all of my views are corroborated, the statute may well have been beneficial for some women. I simply believed that it would be difficult to apply and would have a limited impact, not all of it beneficial, and that these aspects of the EPA should be investigated. I believe that this volume confirms my views, but readers will ultimately judge that for themselves.

PROCEDURE AND PURPOSES

The primary method used for this study of the EPA is that of critiquing the court decisions made under the Act. I have read most, if not all, of the published decisions of the federal courts on cases brought under the statute. In general, I read the court opinions from the perspective of whether they made sense—equitable, economic, and otherwise. More precisely, my assessments were guided in the main by three criteria: the extent to which the court decisions followed the language of the statute as that language was informed by evidence of Congressional intent; the soundness of the reasoning that produced the decisions and its consistency with other decisions; and the equity, economic, and other ramifications of the decisions.

This method, of course, is a limited form of empiricism that cannot possibly produce a complete answer to the question of how the statute has worked. I have not attempted to measure the impacts of the EPA on women generally, male workers, employers, or the economy. My method can get at those impacts only rather obliquely, by observing the behavior that the courts have ruled to be permissible and prohibited under the Act, and by making inferences about the larger impacts of those rulings. Obviously, this procedure cannot produce quantitative assessments and, perhaps, not even qualitative ones that have wide generality and are verifiable. Yet, I believe that much can be learned about the workings of the EPA through review of the court rulings that it has produced and through reasoned inferences about how employers (and unions), who were the essential target of the law, have been affected by these rulings and the Act generally. Whether this view is correct is of some interest itself, because this particular combination of empiricism and theorizing, while not novel, has not been widely employed to assess the effects of social legislation.

It may be useful to state here how I perceive the connections between this study of the Equal Pay Act and the so-called "comparable worth" notion of pay equity that is now advocated in some, largely female, quarters.[2] Comparable worth advocates contend that the wage rates for "female" jobs are low precisely because the jobs predominately employ women; thus, the low wages are inconsistent with the skills and responsibilities of these jobs and are discriminatory. The remedy for this discrimination is to raise the wage rates for female jobs to levels that accurately reflect their "worth" in relation to that of nonfemale jobs, as that worth is determined through job evaluation or some other means. Part of the effort to implement this view has been directed to the courts, attempting to persuade them that the low wage rates for certain female jobs are, indeed, discriminatory and, as such, violate Title VII of the 1964 Civil Rights Act, which comprehensively prohibits employment discrimination. To date, the courts have not responded affirmatively, but they will undoubtedly have additional opportunities to do so.*

There are several connections between the EPA and the comparable-worth view. First, the legislation that ultimately became the EPA, introduced in Congress 1962, prohibited unequal pay for "comparable work." Subsequently, the ban was changed to "equal work," presumably reflecting the views of Congressmembers and their constituents that the government ought not to regulate wage setting for jobs that could not be easily compared. Second, under the EPA there have been attempts to enlarge the inter-

---

*The decision of the U.S. Supreme Court in *County of Washington vs. Gunther*, 452 U.S. 161 (1981), opened the door to the *possibility* of comparable worth litigation. This matter is discussed in Chapter 8.

pretation of equal work to encompass more of a comparable work standard. The courts have rejected these attempts. Third, because of the wording of the EPA, a limited form of comparable-worth job comparison does occur under the statute. This will be described in Chapter 5 and may shed some light on the current debate. Finally, the EPA attempts to regulate wage setting under certain narrow circumstances, as would the comparable-worth view under more general circumstances. In Chapter 8, I discuss the developing law of comparable worth and show how court decisions that have been made under the EPA are likely to restrain that development. Thus, I believe that this study will provide illumination relevant to the current debate about comparable worth wage setting.

In a larger sense, this book can be looked upon as a case study relevant to the proposition that has been the principal guide for federal governance of the U.S. for the last fifty years, the proposition that government regulation can improve the overall welfare of the citizenry. While still enjoying considerable support, that proposition has come under severe attack in recent years. My examination of the EPA, which is social reform legislation, provides a bit of evidence for a debate that will go on for many more years. Thus, it is my hope that this study will be useful for those interested in the question of whether social reform legislation works, as well as for those who must decide whether particular work practices are consistent with the EPA.

The next chapter deviates from the method of inquiry described here and used for the remainder of the book; it examines in theory and fact the need for the EPA, based on the premise that this need, or its absence, has influenced judicial applications of the Act. Chapter 3 presents an overview of the statute and the issues that have arisen under it. Chapter 4 describes three important EPA cases in some detail. Chapter 5 examines the courts' rather unsuccessful attempts to operationalize the concept of equal work. Chapter 6 considers market defenses for unequal pay, and Chapter 7 examines the influence of Title VII of the 1964 Civil Rights Act on the EPA, concluding that the former has a dominant influence on equal work decisions under the latter. Chapter 8 connects EPA law with the developing law of comparable worth, and the final chapter presents some facts about EPA enforcement and summarizes my conclusions.

NOTES

1. 29 U.S. Code 206 (d) (1).

2. See, for example, Ruth Blumrosen, "Wage Discrimination, Job Segregation and Title VII of the Civil Rights Act of 1964," *University of Michigan Journal of Law Reform* 12 (1979): 397.

2

THE DEMAND FOR EQUAL PAY:
BACKGROUND OF THE EPA

The social demand for equal pay for women has a long history that will not be traced here. In general, there have been two motivations behind the demand: justice for women workers, and protection of the jobs and wages of men.

The concern with justice for women workers arose out of their low earnings, generally, as well as from specific instances where they replaced men, or were employed alongside them, at a lower wage than that paid to men. This concern was given considerable impetus in the 1960s by the increasing participation of women in the labor force, an increase in divorces which made women, and sometimes their children, dependent solely on their own earnings from employment; and an increase in societal sensitivity to demands for social justice. The latter aided the quest for female equality by drawing attention to the low earnings and limited job opportunities of women, especially compared to those of white males.

The historically more important motivation behind the drive for equal pay has been the desire of male workers to protect themselves from female competition.[1] Since the industrial revolution, females have been a threat to low-skilled male workers. The threat has been that women would replace male workers because the former could be hired at lower wage rates, or that women would force reductions in male wages to meet competition from goods and services produced by lower paid females.

Trade unions, particularly conscious of job scarcity, have often led equal pay efforts to remove these threats.[2] Their participation has been grounded in the general union philosophy of "equal pay for equal work," which has had a broader objective than that of equal pay for women. The unions' objective has been to equalize wage rates, and thus labor costs to firms, for all union members (and other workers, if possible) who are performing the same job, regardless of the firm or geographic area in which they are employed. When successful, this policy eliminates competition between firms based upon price cutting made possible by low wage rates. It therefore means that the job security of union members in any firm cannot be threatened by low wage rates paid to workers in other firms. Union support for statutory minimum wages is based upon this philosophy, as is union support for equal pay for women. A statutory requirement of equal pay for women dictates that employers cannot replace men with lower paid women. It therefore provides job protection for male workers.

Of course, to the extent that the requirement of equal pay for women protects male workers, it also reduces job opportunities for women. Many supporters of women's rights, including feminists, seem oblivious to this fact, or else attach little importance to it compared to the value, symbolic or otherwise, of achieving equality of pay for women who do the same work as men.

Although feminists have long demanded equal wages for women, some early activists for women's rights had misgivings about this goal because they saw that its achievement would reduce female job opportunities. The English female advocate, Millicent G. Fawcett, was initially critical of the equal-pay-for-equal-work principle because she thought it would exclude women from employment where they were likely to be less efficient than men.[3] Later she defended the equal pay slogan but in its implementation called for "a pro rata reduction in their standard rates. . .for any permanent disadvantage that adheres to women workers as such."[4]

Another early twentieth century British activist, Eleanor F. Rathbone, called for a policy of free entry to all occupations for women and pay proportionate to output. This writer believed that women would be excluded from many jobs unless they insisted "that the rates of pay which they are permitted to accept shall be sufficiently lower than men's rates to balance, but not more than balance, the inherent disadvantages of female labour."[5]

The connection between equal pay for women and male job protection can be seen through the timing of equal pay demands. Before the passage of the EPA in 1963, those demands were greatest in the U.S. during World Wars I and II, when women were hired in considerable numbers for jobs formerly held only by males. (The equal pay movement during World War II may also have been strengthened by a practice prevalent during the immediately preceding Great Depression: that of replacing men with women who entered the labor market because their husbands had lost their jobs or had been reduced to part-time work.[6]) Michigan and Montana passed equal pay laws just after World War I, and four other industrial states enacted them during World War II. Support for the policy of equal pay was widespread in World War II, coming from government, labor, and management, although considerably less from management than the other two.

These institutional groups were dominated by males, of course, and a *Columbia Law Review* note just after the war opined that "The objective of full male employment may account for the widespread acceptance of the policy of equal pay. . . ."[7]

More than anything else, it was the experience of the National War Labor Board (WLB) in promulgating its "equal pay" policy during World War II that led to the introduction of equal pay bills in Congress in 1945 and subsequent years. The Board's famous General Order No. 16, issued in November 1942, authorized equal pay to women "for comparable quality and quantity of work on the same or similar operations."[8] The WLB was conservative in applying this policy, refusing to apply it to jobs that were not similar and permitting sexual wage differentials based on ascertainable productivity and cost differences. Nevertheless, it did equalize male and female wage rates in many firms where women replaced men or were employed in jobs previously reserved for men.[9]

Despite the experiences of the WLB and the widespread support that existed for its "equal pay" policy, a federal equal pay law was not enacted in World War II or the immediate postwar years. Not until 1963, following great increases in female employment and the revival of concern with social issues that accompanied the Kennedy Administration, was such a law enacted.

THE NEED FOR THE ACT

The apparent reasons for the passage of the EPA were twofold: the average earnings of women workers in the U.S., in 1963 as today, were less than 60 percent of those of men; and many people believed that a significant number of women were doing the same work as that done by men but were being paid less for it. There can be no argument about the reality of low earnings for women. However, it is also true that those earnings are not, and have never been, due principally to unequal pay for equal work; rather, they result from the concentration of female employment in low-wage jobs. A large proportion of female employment has long been in nursing, teaching, clerical, and low-level sales and service positions. None of these occupations pay comparatively well. One investigator of male-female wage differences concluded: "In my opinion, most of the 40 percentage points [difference between male and female average hourly earnings] can be explained by the different roles assigned to men and women. . . . We have not found. . .evidence that employer discrimination is a major direct influence upon male-female differentials in average hourly earnings."[10]

The EPA may well owe its existence to the low wages of women. However, it focused on obtaining better (equal) wages for women who were doing *equal* work; it made no attempt to remedy a problem stemming from the fact that women were doing *different* work.

The second reason for passage of the Act, the apparent belief that many women were doing equal work for less pay, was not well founded in either theory or fact. To show that well-intentioned legislation, such as the EPA, is sometimes directed to problems that are more apparent than real, it is necessary to examine the theoretical and empirical bases for this belief in some detail.

Theory

In the introduction, I cited two reasons for believing that unequal pay for equal work within a single establishment, the focus of the Act, was uncommon when the statute was passed in 1963: (1) the personnel practice of permitting wage differentiation among employees engaged in the same work risks employee unrest unless the differences are based upon seniority or observable differences in job performance; (2) unequal pay for equal work is inefficient since wage costs could be reduced by paying only the lower wage and hiring all females (unless males also apply at the lower wage). Both reasons must be qualified.

The notion that the morale of at least some employees will be adversely affected by a dual wage system is a generally sound postulate of modern personnel administration. It arises from a desire to attract and retain high quality employees and a belief that equitable pay practices will help in this regard. There are employers, however, who for one reason or other do not need to be concerned about employee unrest and morale. They may have a work force that is without employment alternatives (monopsony), or employee morale and the possibility of employee turnover are of no importance to them because replacement workers are readily available. Such employers can maintain dual wage rates for men and women without fear of employee reactions.

There is a more important reason for believing that unequal pay for equal work is uncommon: even if an employer is willing to risk the employee unrest that likely accompanies this practice, it does not make business sense to employ men to perform work at one wage rate while employing women to do the same work at a lower wage. Any profit-maximizing or cost-minimizing employer would want to change these circumstances to get all the work done at the lower wage. Perhaps only women would be employed at the lower wage, or perhaps some men would also accept it. Regardless, only one wage—that necessary to employ enough workers, men or women—would be paid for the work.

By this economic logic, which says that markets generally produce a single price for a given product, one might conclude that there cannot be unequal pay rates for equal work. That conclusion is too strong, however, because under certain conditions equal work with unequal pay for women can exist or at least appear to exist. The more important of these conditions are:

1.   *The greater cost of employing women.* If the employment costs of women systematically exceed those of men, due, for example, to greater use of sick leave, a lower wage for women can equate the unit labor costs—wage and other employment costs per unit of output—of the two sexes and make an employer willing to employ both men and women for equal work (assuming no problem of employee unrest). In such circumstances, women will not be employed unless they can be paid less than men.

2.   *The lower productivity of women.* If the productivity of women is systematically below that of men for certain work, a lower wage for women could, again, equalize the unit labor costs of the two groups and bring about the employment of both sexes on a given job at unequal wage rates.

3.   *The expectation of job advancement by men but not women.* If men on a given job are seen as promotable to higher positions and women are not, an employer would be willing to pay men more than women if this were necessary to employ men with qualifications for future advancement. In essence, the male workers are providing something beyond simply their work output—the possibility of greater output in the future. The employer is willing to pay for this extra contribution, to pay for training costs, so to speak. The exclusion of women from training and promotion opportunities is unlawful today, but it was not when the EPA was passed.

4.   *An insufficient supply of women.* If there are not enough women to fill all the available jobs, an employer may hire some men and pay them a higher wage than the women.[4] This dual wage system could not occur in a competitive labor market, however, because employers would bid up wages for women until they equaled those of men. Monospony labor markets—those that include only one or a very few employers—are not sufficiently widespread to bring about much unequal pay for equal work.

5.   *Collective bargaining agreements.* EPA court cases show that some union-employer contracts provided unequal pay for equal, or nearly equal, work at the time of the statute's enactment. These arrangements were most likely the result of union willingness to permit only limited employment of women at a lower wage and employer willingness to guarantee a certain amount or proportion of employment to males. In short, these agreements provided lower wage costs for employers and increased job security to certain male union members.

6.   *Bona fide "male" and "female" jobs.* A small number of jobs are divided into male and female positions because of prevailing mores. One ex-

ample is the job of retail clothing salesperson, where the work tasks of salesmen and saleswomen are essentially the same but customer preferences, or at least employer beliefs about customer preferences, produce sex segregation in work assignments. (This segregation is diminishing but still exists, for example, in the selling of suits.) Under these circumstances men may receive a higher rate of pay than women who are doing equal work in the same establishment, because employers believe that customer preferences would make it unprofitable to replace salesmen with lower paid saleswomen. In other words, labor market competition cannot produce a single wage for a clothing salesperson, regardless of sex, because existing mores work against it. The number of jobs falling into this category is very small and diminishing as sexual mores change and employers look for ways to reduce their labor costs (see, for example, the increase in the number of female sportswriters). Note that a societal belief, right or wrong, that a woman cannot perform a certain job does not ordinarily produce unequal pay for equal work but rather results in the exclusion of women from the job altogether—from coal mining, for example.

Collectively, these hypothetical employment conditions suggest there was some unequal pay for equal work in 1963, but they do not suggest a widespread incidence, since the necessary employment conditions did not exist frequently, even in 1963. Although hearings on equal pay legislation in 1963 produced employer testimony that women are more costly to employ than men, these views were contested, and no evidence was presented to show that unequal pay based on sexual differences in employment costs was common.[12] The productivity of males and females is probably similar for most jobs; where it differs, the sex with the greater productivity tends to dominate employment so that male-female job integration with dual pay rates within an establishment is rare. EPA court decisions of 1963 indicate many instances in which men were paid more than women for equal work because the former were considered to be in training programs for future job advancement. However, the Act permits this kind of unequal pay as long as the training program is *bona fide* rather than a pretext for wage discrimination. The major problem with training programs in 1963 was not unequal pay but that they were often not available to women; Title VII attempted to remedy that inequity in 1964.

The leading sources of unequal pay for equal work in 1963 were probably collective bargaining agreements and the existence of male and female categories for the same job. Collective bargaining agreements enforced the employment of both sexes on substantially equal jobs for unequal wage rates, whereas, in the absence of such agreements, the competitive process would have replaced men with lower paid women or equalized the wage rates of the two sexes. It is doubtful, however, that collective agreements providing for unequal pay covered more than a very small fraction of all female employment. Male and female categories of the same job, with sex a *bona fide* qualification for each category, are rare today but were more common in pre-Title VII days. In 1963, some unequal pay for equal work was maintained by the mores of sex segregation.

Note that three of the employment conditions cited—the higher employment cost of women, their lower productivity, and their exclusion from training programs—are not only uncommon, but also, where they do exist, produce only the *appearance* and not the reality of unequal pay for equal work. Under these conditions, unequal pay simply equalizes employment costs per production unit (over the long run, in the case of training programs) for men and women. The EPA recognized this fact by providing certain exceptions to the equal pay requirement. Consistent differences in the employment costs, productivity, and training participation of men and women all fall under the broad "factor-other-than-sex" exception of the statute: they constitute justifiable grounds for paying unequal wages for what appears, on the surface, to be equal work. In practice, however, the higher cost and lower productivity defenses are almost never used, because the courts have held that the higher cost or lower productivity must be shown for each *individual* female employee.[13]

On the other hand, to the extent that unequal pay was based on *erroneous* beliefs about female employment costs, their productivity, or their suitability for training programs, the EPA did meet an important need to revise these beliefs. All the same, it must be remembered that these erroneous beliefs cost employers money. If a sexual wage difference is based on an inaccurate belief about male-female productivity differences, for example, the employer has an incentive to discover the truth and replace men with lower paid but equally productive women.

In theory, then the EPA was needed to remedy conditions of unequal pay (1) under collective bargaining agreements; (2) for male and female categories of the same job; and (3) based on erroneous views about the cost, productivity, or training suitability of women. These possible bases for unequal pay do not suggest a great need for the law, particularly considered in light of the personnel administration principle that employee morale and job performance can be harmed by inequitable pay practices. Rather than pay different wages to men and women for the same work and risk antagonizing at least the female employees, an employer is likely to set one rate for the job. (This is true even where the employment costs or productivities of the two sexes do in fact differ.) If the rate is set low, the employer may wind up employing only females. If it is set high, the employer may be able to hire only men if that is preferred. A nondiscriminating employer who pays the higher rate will hire both men and women, selected on the basis of their individual qualifications.

Put succinctly, except under extraordinary circumstances, unequal pay for equal work is not viable because it is a visible inequity and because employers have an economic incentive to replace higher paid workers with lower paid ones. I conclude from these theoretical considerations that undoubtedly some women were receiving unequal pay for equal work in 1963 when the EPA was enacted but that the proportion of all women workers in this status was very small. In the next section, this conclusion will be checked against the available facts.

Evidence: World War II

Congressional hearings on equal pay legislation were conducted in the years immediately following World War II. Legislation was not enacted, however, and interest in this matter waned until 1962. Hearings were resumed in that year and in 1963, when the EPA was passed. Records of these hearings and other sources suggest that considerable unequal pay for equal work was generated as the nation increased its production capacity for the war. Much of this practice was eliminated during the war, and by the time of EPA enactment the incidence of this inequity was not widespread.

Before World War II, men and women workers were not usually employed on the same job. Even during World War I ". . .the American labor force had two separate work and wage tracks—one for men and another for women."[14] This job segregation was based largely on widely held stereotypes of female and male roles in the U.S. economy and society. Women were thought to be less productive than men for many jobs. They were viewed as short-term workers who would eventually marry and leave the labor force for household obligations. They were thought to need less income than men, who were assumed to be supporting families. As a consequence of these views, most women were confined to "light" occupations that involved low pay and little training (unless they paid for the training themselves, as in teaching and nursing). Unions, where they existed, usually supported this pattern of employment by resisting employer efforts to make use of the female labor supply.[15]

This employment pattern was broken rather rapidly in the war industries once World War II began. In fact, it had begun to change earlier during the Great Depression, when women, attempting to replace the earnings of their unemployed husbands, were hired for factory work by employers seeking to reduce their labor costs. Unequal pay was often the major incentive for hiring these women. For example, men earning 45-50 cents an hour were replaced by women earning 25-30 cents in parts of the Michigan automobile industry during the 1930s.[16]

Women in General Motors' Oldsmobile plant, located in Lansing, Michigan, filed charges under the state's equal pay law in 1938. The court eventually awarded them nearly $56,000 in wages due for work periods back to 1932.[17]

Labor shortages quickly developed at the outbreak of World War II because of the expanded war production and loss of workers to the military, and it became necessary to employ women in jobs that they had not held previously. In some instances women completely took over a job class that had been all male; in others, they worked along with men at jobs from which they had previously been excluded. In still other cases, a previously all-male job was changed to eliminate certain heavy or skilled tasks, and women were employed for the diluted position.[18]

Many of the firms that increased their employment of women at this time had separate wage scales that provided lower wage rates for "female" jobs. When women began to be assigned to formerly male jobs, some of these firms continued to pay women at the lower female rates, thus creating pay inequities.

A survey of 62 firms conducted in November 1941, before the U.S. entrance into the war, disclosed that only 17 of them paid the "rate for the job" irrespective of sex.[19] On the other hand, a number of firms quickly adopted a rate-for-the-job pay policy during World War II, if they had not done so earlier. The aircraft and steel industries appeared to lead in this regard.[20]

It is not possible to be precise about the incidence of inequitable pay practices during World War II, either for women who had replaced men or for women performing the same or similar work as men. A significant number of firms did engage in these practices, but from the available evidence, it appears that they were a minority of all employers.

A survey of New York war industries found that 60 percent of the 514 plants that had replaced men with women paid equal entrance wages to the two sexes.[21] A U.S. Women's Bureau survey in 1943 found that 87 percent of the 224 war plants surveyed reported a "pay for the job" policy.[22]

Spearheaded by the National War Labor Board policy of one rate for the job, there was a major movement toward abolishing wage differentials based on sex during World War II.[23] As mentioned earlier, the Board's General Order No. 16, issued in November 1942, authorized employers to raise wage rates for females who were being paid less than males "for comparable quality and quantity of work on the same or similar operations." Such wage adjustments could be made without Board approval. Over two thousand employers reported these voluntary wage increases between November 1942 and January 1944, showing both the existence of unequal pay practices at the beginning of the war and the elimination of many such practices during the war.[24] Many employers, in fact, urged the WLB to adopt an equal pay policy so that they could raise female wage rates and attract badly needed women workers.[25]

The practice of job evaluation, also encouraged by the WLB, increased greatly during and after World War II. The National Industrial Conference Board reported that 13 percent of firms surveyed in 1939 used this technique, compared to 57 percent in 1947.[26] Job evaluation is antithetical to unequal pay for equal work because it ordinarily produces one wage rate for a job regardless of who performs it. Although some employers set lower wage rates for female dominated jobs that were evaluated as equal to those of males, this appears not to have occurred when men and women were performing work of substantially the same task content.[27] The latter was the focus of the 1963 EPA; thus, job evaluation reduced the incidence of the unequal pay to which the Act was directed.

The 1960s

Despite its success during World War II, a federal equal pay policy could not be enacted in the immediate postwar years. This legislation was not again considered seriously until it was supported by the Kennedy Administration in 1962, seventeen years after the war's end. By then, women were one-third of the total labor force, compared to about one-fourth in 1945, and although the more militant feminist efforts had not yet begun, there was no doubt that women were an increasingly important component of the nation's work force. Ironically, the need for an equal pay statute appears to have declined over this period due to the continued growth of sophisticated personnel practices, led by job evaluation; the continued segregation of men and women into different jobs; and the pursuit of equal pay policies by trade unions.[28]

The evidence presented at the Congressional hearings on the EPA in 1962 and 1963, principally by the U.S. Department of Labor, did not convincingly substantiate the inequity that the Act was designed to eliminate: unequal pay for equal work *within a single business establishment.*[29] Many facts were presented on the low earnings of women compared to men, generally, and on the comparatively low-paying jobs held by the former, but this evidence was not germane to the very speicifc focus of the EPA. Evidence presented on the different average earnings of men and women employed in certain narrowly defined urban occupations was relevant to the general principle of equal pay for equal work but not to the narrow purview of that principle—the business establishment—to which the proposed legislation was limited.

In contrast to the earlier postwar hearings, comparatively little anecdotal evidence about unequal pay practices in industry was presented in the 1962–63 hearings. Some evidence submitted by officials of unions or women's organizations tended to miss the point of the proposed legislation because it dealt with the inferior jobs held by women and the low pay received for these jobs. Also, some of the testimony dealt with comparable rather than equal work; certain employers, General Electric and Westinghouse, for example, apparently paid women less for work that was different from that done by men but equal in terms of job evaluations.[30]

The facts that the Department of Labor submitted about *establishment* pay practices, the appropriate focus of the evidence, can be summarized as follows:

1. Job orders submitted by employers to public employment offices which listed higher hiring rates for men than for women. Ninety-one examples of such orders were found in the public employment offices of nine cities in 1963. One-third of these provided a wage differential of 10 percent or less (of the male wage); one-half contained a differential of 10–25 percent.[31]

2. Responses from two national surveys of employer pay practices. Thirty-three percent of the employer respondents in one survey indicated that they had a "double standard pay scale for male and female office workers." Eighty-three percent of the respondents in the second survey said that they "always pay the same" salary to women and men for their management positions. The remainder "sometimes" paid the same salary.[32]

3. Statistics from establishments in twenty labor markets showing the differences in weekly earnings between men and women for nine occupations.[33] The statistics are summarized in Table 2-1.

4. A list of the 14 (out of 792) U.S. school districts that reported higher salary schedules for male than female teachers for the 1962–63 school year.[34]

An additional piece of evidence submitted by the Department of Labor, inadvertently or otherwise, tended to minimize the extent of inequitable pay practices. This evidence, consisting of establishment pay practices for seven factory occupations in twenty-nine machinery centers, is reproduced in Table 2-2. The commentary that accompanied this table stated ". . .that different distributions of men and women workers within an established range [due to job tenure differences] might account for from 5 to 10 cents of the total difference in men's and women's earnings."[35] That being so, the table indicates that women's earnings were at least equal to those of men in a majority of establishments for all seven occupations.

Although this evidence suggests the existence of some unequal pay for equal work prior to enactment of the EPA, it does not show that this inequity was either widespread or an important contributor to the low earnings of

Table 2-1

Percent of Establishments in Which Average Weekly Earnings of Men Exceeded Those of Women by $1 or More, Labor Markets, 1958–59

Occupation	Percent of Establishments
Accounting clerks, Class A	65
Accounting clerks, Class B	56
Order clerks	71
Payroll clerks	62
Office boys or girls	41
Tabulating machine operators	54
Janitors, porters, and cleaners*	72
Packers, shipping*	70
Elevator operators, passenger*	32

*Percent of establishments in which average hourly earnings of men exceeded those of women by 3 cents or more.

Source: U.S. Bureau of Labor Statistics, Bull. No. 1240-22, *Wages and Related Benefits, 20 Labor Markets, 1958–59,* p. 45.

women generally. Perhaps the most important evidence, that dealing with average earnings differences within establishments (Table 2-1), was flawed by the failure to adjust earnings for differences in job tenure between men and women. This adjustment is necessary since so many firms reward length of service with increased pay, and the average job tenure of men is greater than that of women. In 1966, the median years on the same job were 5.2 for males and 2.8 for females.[36] Sex differences in occupational levels undoubtedly accounted for some of this difference. The Department of Labor commentary on these statistics noted that differences in job content and job tenure "at least partially" accounted for the pay differences shown, but this did not stop the Department from submitting the data to the House and Senate committees as evidence of unequal pay for equal work.[37]

Statistics published by the U.S. Bureau of Labor Statistics subsequent to enactment of the EPA tend to support the conclusion that unequal pay for equal work was of little importance to the overall welfare of women workers in the mid-1960s. The statistics in Table 2-3 show that the median establishment difference between male and female earnings in a nationwide

Table 2–2

Percent of Establishments with Lower Average Earnings for Women than for Men Plant Workers, Twenty-nine Machinery Centers, 1952–53

Occupation	Percent of Establishments in which Women's Average Earnings Were—		
	Lower Than Men's	Lower by Over 5 Cents	Lower by Over 10 Cents
Assemblers, Class B	68	47	26
Assemblers, Class C	70	50	30
Inspectors, Class B	70	44	20
Inspectors, Class C	65	47	36
Drill press operators (single or multiple spindle), Class C	42	32	19
Grinding machine operators, Class C	42	17	17
Milling machine operators, Class C	44	33	11

Source: U.S. Department of Labor, Bureau of Labor Statistics. Data reproduced from U.S. Senate, Subcommittee on Labor, Committee on Labor and Public Welfare, *Hearings: Equal Pay Act of 1963,* 88th Congress, 1963, p. 27.

sample was rather small—five percent or less for all but one of the twelve occupations covered—and was nonexistent for some occupations. Furthermore, all but the largest of the earnings differences shown in Table 2–3 can probably be accounted for by sex differences in job tenure and content. Since the figures shown were obtained in 1965–66, one to two years after the EPA became law (its effective date was June 11, 1964, except where existing collective bargaining agreements extended to June 11, 1965, in which case the latter was the effective date), it can be argued that they were influenced by compliance with the law. It seems unlikely, however, that the law would significantly narrow sexual wage differences in such a brief period of time.

By way of contrast, Table 2–3 also presents average earnings differences between all male and female workers in the survey for the occupa-

Table 2-3
Male-Female Wage Differences By Occupation
Within Establishments and for All Men and Women, 1965-66

	Median Establishment Difference (Percent: M-F) Between Average Earnings of Men and Women	Percent by Which Average Weekly Earnings of All Men Exceeded Those of All Women
Office (weekly earnings)		
Clerks, accounting Class A	3	19
Clerks, accounting Class B	3	23
Clerks, order	15	36
Clerks, payroll	3	26
Office boys or girls	−4 to 6	5
Tabulating machine operator		
Class A	−3 to 3	8
Class B	−2	10
Class C	−4	6
Plant (hourly earnings)		
Janitors, porters, & cleaners	5	17
Packers, shipping	1	22

Source: Donald J. McNulty, "Differences in Pay Between Men and Women Workers," *Monthly Labor Review* 90, December 1967, pp. 40–43.

tions shown. These differences are much larger than those that existed within establishments, demonstrating that, even for narrowly defined occupations, male-female earnings differences are explained principally by the employment of men in higher paying establishments, rather than by unequal pay within establishments.

Ex post facto support for the conclusion that unequal pay for equal work was relatively unimportant when the EPA was passed is provided by a study showing little change in male-female earnings differentials between 1960 and 1970 for the occupations shown in Table 2-3.* The author of this report concluded: "It is difficult to observe from these data any consistent effect resulting from the Equal Pay Act."[38]

In sum, the empirical evidence tends to support the theoretical reasoning: there was no great need for the EPA when it was passed in 1963; little of the difference in earnings between men and women was due to establishment practices of unequal pay for equal work. Such practices had been much more common at the start of World War II as women began to be hired for previously all-male jobs. The war appears to have been a transition period during which the need to employ women in traditionally male jobs convinced many employers and unions alike to adopt the rate-for-the-job principle. The equal pay policy of the National War Labor Board helped significantly in this regard.

CONGRESSIONAL SUPPORT FOR THE EPA

Judging from the absence of opposition, the EPA of 1963 certainly manifested an idea whose time had arrived. However, much of the support for the legislation came because its purpose and scope were so modest, especially in comparison to Title VII of the Civil Rights Act which was to be enacted the following year. The Kennedy Administration had sponsored equal pay legislation in 1962 that called for equal pay for "comparable" work. The bill that passed a year later narrowed the equal pay requirement to that of "equal" work. A social awakening to civil rights sensitivities was well underway by 1963. Few members of Congress saw reason to question legislation that incorporated into law the equitable principle that men and women should receive the same pay for equal work. The EPA passed overwhelmingly in May of 1963.

The discussion of the Act in the House of Representatives (the Senate hardly debated it) before its passage was devoted largely to assuring the Act's few opponents that it was (1) narrow in scope, and (2) could not be used by the U.S. Department of Labor to harass business establishments. The bill's supporters went to some excesses on the first point, assuring the House members that equal pay would be required only when men and women were performing the "same job under the same working conditions," or "virtually identical" jobs.[39] These adjectival criteria were more limiting than that of "equal" work, the adjective actually included in the Act.

The House discussion referred only very briefly to the possible impact of the bill on female job opportunities. Congressman Findlay (Ill.) cited a

---

*Male–female earnings differences *within establishments* are not available for 1960; however, the article cited shows that they, also, failed to narrow from 1965–70.

possible decline in those opportunities as the major reason for his unsuccessful amendment that would have permitted a wage differential reflecting the "ascertainable and specific" added cost of employing a woman.[40] A more revealing comment was made by Congressman Goodell (N.Y.), whose own equal pay bill formed much of the basis for the legislation that finally passed. Goodell was the minority floor manager of the legislation and the leading contributor to the floor debate. At one point he made the following statement:

> . . .I think there will be a boomerang effect in this legislation. There may be a stampeding back to the nest. I think many of the women advocating this legislation recognize that in some instances the women are going to lose their jobs because an employer has to pay the women the same price he pays the men. In many other cases the woman will just not be hired.[41]

One can infer from these words that "many of the women advocating" the EPA were willing to accept reduced job opportunities for women in return for equitable wages for those who remained employed. Alternatively, female supporters of the Act may have disagreed with the view that some employers would not hire women if they had to pay them as much as men. (Goodell's vision of a "stampeding back to the nest" was certainly wrong.) Regardless, it was evident from both the House debate and the committee hearings that two motives were present when the EPA was passed: equitable pay for women, and reduced job competition between men and women. One can only wonder about the relative force of these two motives.

SUMMARY

The EPA was enacted against a backdrop of national embarrassment and inequity: the average earnings of female workers in the U.S. were only 60 percent of those received by males. Yet the legislation passed by Congress was an extremely cautious and limited approach to this phenomenon, directed only to unequal pay for substantially the same work when performed by men and women within individual establishments. It did not touch the problems of women's limited access to jobs or the low pay for occupations they were able to enter. Indeed, there was not even a substantial need to remedy the situation to which the law was directed—unequal pay for equal work within establishments.

This is not to say that the EPA should not have been passed. Undoubtedly, there were many instances of unequal pay that the Act could remedy, even though these remedies would have little impact in the aggregate. Further the Act had important symbolic value because it directed public policy against a fundamental injustice to women, and it may have also provided hope to many women who needed it that stronger measures aimed at improving the treatment of women would follow.

Nonetheless, the absence of a clearcut need for the EPA did affect its implementation by the government and the courts. Faced with a problem of uncertain, but certainly very small, dimensions unequal pay litigation was brought, sometimes successfully, against employment practices that were probably not covered by Congressional intent when Congress passed the Act. This litigation will be examined in subsequent chapters.

NOTES

1. Dorothy S. Brady, "Equal Pay for Women Workers," *Annals* 251 (1947):53.

2. Eleanor F. Rathbone, "The Remuneration of Women's Service," *Economic Journal* 27 (1917):56.

3. Millicent G. Fawcett, "A Living Wage," *Economic Journal* 4 (1894):366.

4. Millicent G. Fawcett, "Equal Pay for Equal Work," *Economic Journal* 28 (1918):2.

5. Rathbone, op. cit., p. 64.

6. Brady, op. cit., p. 54.

7. "Equal Pay for Equal Work," *Columbia Law Review* 46 (1946):442.

8. Ella J. Polinsky, "National War Labor Board Policy on Equal Pay for Equal Work for Women," in U.S. Senate, *Hearings: Equal Pay for Equal Work for Women*, 79th Congress, 1st Session (1945):41.

9. Ibid., 211-52.

10. Victor R. Fuchs, "Differences in Hourly Earnings Between Men and Women," *Monthly Labor Review* 94, 5 (1971):14.

11. P. Sargent Florence, "A Statistical Contribution to the Theory of Women's Wages," *Economic Journal* 41 (1931):19-37.

12. U.S. Senate, Subcommittee on Labor, Committee on Labor and Public Welfare, *Hearings: Equal Pay Act of 1963*, 88th Congress, 1st Session (1963):141-3, 163, 167.

13. See *Wirtz v. Midwest Manufacturing Co.*, 58 CCH LC 32070, (S.D. ILL. 1968); 29 *U.S. Code of Fed. Reg.* 800.151 (1982).

14. Maurine Weiner Greenwald, *Women, War and Work* (Westport, Conn.: Greenwald Press, 1980) p. 8.

15. Ibid., pp. 158, 178.

16. U.S. Senate, *Hearings*, 1945, op. cit., p. 174.

17. U.S. House of Representatives, Subcommittee No. 4, Committee on Education and Labor, *Hearings: Equal Pay for Equal Work for Women*, 80th Congress, 2nd Session (1948): pp. 113-120.

18. U.S. Senate, *Hearings*, 1945, op. cit., pp. 171, 185.

19. Helen Baker, *Women in War Industries* (Industrial Relations Section, Princeton University, 1942), pp. 44-47.

20. U.S. Senate, *Hearings*, 1945, op. cit., pp. 35–38.

21. "Equal Pay Principle in New York War Industries," *Monthly Labor Review* 57 (1943): 102-4.

22. U.S. Senate, *Hearings*, 1945, op. cit., p. 37.

23. Baker, op. cit., p. 47.

24. U.S. Senate, *Hearings*, 1945, op. cit., p. 10.

25. Ibid.

26. U.S. House of Representatives, *Hearings*, 1948, op. cit., p. 141.

27. Ibid., pp. 31, 200, 246–49.

28. U.S. House of Representatives, Select Subcommittee, Committee on Education and Labor, *Hearings: Equal Pay for Equal Work*, 87th Congress, 2nd Session (1962): 162–64.

29. See U.S. House of Representatives, *Hearings*, 1962, op. cit.; U.S. Senate, Subcommittee on Labor, Committee on Labor and Public Welfare, *Hearings: Equal Pay Act of 1962*, 87th Congress, 2nd Session (1962); U.S. Senate, *Hearings*, 1963, op. cit.; U.S. House of Representatives, Select Subcommittee, Committee on Education and Labor, *Hearings: Equal Pay Act*, 88th Congress, 1st Session (1963).

30. U.S. House of Representatives, *Hearings*, 1962, op. cit., pp. 174–176.

31. U.S. Senate, *Hearings*, 1963, op. cit., pp. 24–25.

32. Ibid., p. 27.

33. Ibid., pp. 30, 36–38.

34. Ibid., p. 40.

35. Ibid., p. 26

36. H. R. Hamel, "Job Tenure of Workers, January 1966," *Monthly Labor Review* 90 (1967): 33.

37. U.S. Senate, *Hearings*, 1962, op. cit., p. 69.

38. John E. Buckley, "Pay Differences Between Men and Women in the Same Job," *Monthly Labor Review* 94 (1971):38.

39. *U.S. Congressional Record*, 109:9196-7 (May 23, 1963).

40. Ibid., 9206, 9217.

41. Ibid., 9208.

3

ELEMENTS OF THE EPA

The purpose of this chapter is to lay out the various elements of the equal pay law, emphasizing those that have been most important to the outcomes of cases brought under the statute. This will give the reader a general understanding of the legal issues involved in the law's enforcement and will provide a foundation for the case and detailed law discussions that follow.

OVERVIEW

The Equal Pay Act was passed as an amendment to the Fair Labor Standards Act of 1938. Responsibility for its enforcement fell under the Wage and Hour Division of the U.S. Department of Labor, which also enforces the minimum wage, overtime, and child labor laws. In July, 1979, enforcement responsibility was transferred to the Equal Employment Opportunity Commission, as one step toward the consolidation of anti-discrimination enforcement under the Commission.

The Fair Labor Standards Act authorizes the Secretary of Labor to file suits against employers. Although suits by private plaintiffs have increased, since the mid-1970s, the Secretary has brought most of the litigation that has occurred under the EPA.* The Equal Employment Opportunity Commission has been less active in EPA litigation than the Wage and Hour Division since it took over enforcement of the law. Enforcement of the Act is examined in the concluding chapter.

When a court finds that an employer has violated the EPA, it usually awards back pay to the employees who have been paid unequally, providing

---

*The Department of Labor filed about 530 lawsuits between the effective date of the Act, June 11, 1964, and June 30, 1973. Barbara A. Babcock, et al., *Sex Discrimination and the Law* [Boston: Little, Brown & Co., 1975], p. 440.

them with the inequitable wage differential for as much as three years prior to the violation. Under FLSA provisions, liquidated (double) damages are also paid these employees unless the employer's violation was not willful. The finding of a violation also requires that the wage rate for the lower paid job be raised to that of the higher paid one.

There are two parts to the text of the EPA (given in Chapter 1). First, it prohibits the payment of unequal wages to employees who are doing work equal to that of employees of the opposite sex. Second, it permits exceptions to this prohibition; in other words, the law allows for "legitimate" wage differentials between men and women even when they are doing the same work.

The law's two-part structure guides the presentation of EPA cases. First, the plaintiff, either the government or employees (present or former), attempts to show that the employer is (1) paying unequal wages (2) for equal work performed by women. Then the defendant, the employer, attempts to refute the plaintiff's evidence of unequal pay for equal work; or attempts to show that there are legal nonsexual bases for the wage differential; or, most frequently, does both.

THE MEANING OF EQUAL WORK

The Equal Pay Act prohibits the payment of unequal wages to men and women:

> . . . for equal work on jobs the performance of which requires equal skill, effort, and responsibility, and which are performed under similar working conditions. . . .[1]

The meaning of these words is anything but abundantly clear. Let us first consider the key phrase "equal work."

Interpretation of this phrase is made difficult by the fact that "equal" is commonly used two different ways in our language. One use is synonymous with "same"; for example, when two baseball players have "equal" batting averages. The second use occurs when the things compared are different in one sense but are the same in another dimension; for example, the job tasks of electricians and plumbers differ but may be on the same (equal) level with respect to the skills required for each. (One definition of "equal" provided by *Black's Law Dictionary* is "on the same place or level with respect to efficiency, worth, value, amount or rights.") Which of these two uses of "equal" was intended by Congress cannot be determined with certainty simply by reading the Act.

Nonetheless, if one had to decide which of the two definitions—"same as" or "on the same level as"—is conveyed by the language of the statute, the latter meaning would prevail, for several reasons. First, common usage of the term "equal work" encompasses the second definition. When people talk about "equal work" they usually have in mind job tasks which are equivalent (on the same level) along various dimensions, such as required effort and skill, or social and economic value. Identical tasks are not necessary to the ordinary use of the term. (Where identical tasks are involved, "same" rather than "equal," is the more precise descriptive term.) When ordinary people say that a plumber's work is equal to that of an electrician, they mean something to the effect that the plumber's skill, effort, and responsibility are as great as those of an electrician, although they are not the same skill, effort, and responsibility. In short, most people would agree that two people are performing equal work if one person uses as much skill, effort, and responsibility as the other.

Second, not only lay people, but also experts in job comparisons use "equal" to refer to jobs that are on the same level in terms of skills and other requirements, regardless of whether the work tasks are the same. Under evaluation, two jobs are "equal" if their factor (e.g., skill, effort) point totals are approximately equal, even when their work tasks differ markedly.[3]

Third, the EPA states that for "equal work" to exist under the statute, the jobs compared must require "equal skill, effort, and responsibility." If the "equal work" phrase were interpreted as the "same work," the addition of the "equal skill, effort, and responsibility" requirements would be an awkward redundancy: two jobs which provide the same work obviously have equal skill, effort, and responsibility as well. To make sense of the language—that is, to eliminate the redundancy—the "equal work" phrase must be interpreted as meaning not the "same work," but work that is on the same level; and the "equal skill, effort, and responsibility" phrase must be interpreted as enumerating the work characteristics for which the same level must exist. In other words, the statutory language defining equal work is redundant unless it is interpreted as work on the same level with respect to skill, effort, and responsibility.

If "equal" is interpreted as work *on the same level*, the statute would permit comparisons of different jobs to determine whether they require an equivalent level of skill, effort, and responsibility and are performed under similar working conditions; in current terminology, the comparable worth of different jobs could be examined and judged by the courts. If equal levels of these requirements were found to exist, the jobs would be declared equal under the law and would require equal pay.

Congressional Intent

Without additional information about the meaning of the EPA

language, the above interpretations might well have prevailed in the courts. There is, however, additional information about the prohibitory language that leaves no doubt that a considerably narrower definition of "equal work" was intended by Congress. First, the 1962 equal pay legislation introduced by the Kennedy administration and alternative bills all prohibited unequal pay for "comparable" work, whereas the law ultimately enacted in 1963 applied the prohibition only to "equal" work. Congressman Goodell stressed the importance of this change during the House of Representatives floor debate. In his judgment the change from "comparable" to "equal" substantially shortened the reach of the Act by reducing the requirement for equal pay to jobs which were "virtually identical."[4] Second, the comments made during the House debate, particularly those made by the members of the Special Subcommittee on Labor (Committee on Education and Labor), which had revised the bill prior to its presentation to the full House, showed a Congressional intent of narrowly limiting the construction of the "equal work" term. Congressman Frelinghuysen (N.J.), also a member of the subcommittee, stated: "What we seek is to ensure, where men and women are doing the same job under the same working conditions, that they will receive the same pay."[5] No disagreement with these views was stated, and other contributors to the discussion used similar terms. For example, Congresswoman Boulton (Ohio), speaking in support of the bill, said, "It is a matter of simple justice to pay a woman the same rate as a man when she is performing the same duties."[6]

The discussion displayed the subcommittee members' belief that not only were different jobs, such as those of an inspector and an assembler in a factory, barred from being considered equal, but that the law would also consider unequal two inspector positions where one required complicated inspections and the other cursory.[7] While "equal" may be an ambiguous term when applied to work, the House illustrated an intent to define "equal" as meaning nearly "the same as," and thus, not to define it as meaning "on the same level."

Economic View

A third light can be cast on the meaning of equal work by an economic interpretation. Over thirty years ago, the British economist, E. H. Phelps Brown, wrote that two people are doing equal work if their productivity is the same, their costs of employment are the same, and they appear to have the same future value to their employer as assessed through the employment tenure and promotions anticipated for each.[8] The application of this definition is limited, however, because economic doctrine does not provide a useful means of assessing the relative productivity of workers doing different jobs in the production process—an assembler and a shipping clerk, for example.*

These economic principles can be helpful when comparing substantially similar jobs in terms of output. Notice, however, that under the statute they would be relevant only for showing possible exceptions to the requirement of equal pay and could say nothing on the question of whether two jobs actually involve equal work. The latter must be decided entirely on the basis of the job content.

Different costs, productivity, and suitability for training programs constitute exceptions to the requirement of equal pay but must be shown for individuals rather than for each sex as a group. The courts established this principle early in the EPA litigation when they ruled that the law does not permit individuals to be treated as members of their sex group for purposes of ascribing the group's average costs to the individual.[9]

Court Conclusions

Although court decisions defining equal work will be discussed in some detail in Chapter 5, the reader may wish to know at this point the general direction that these decisions have taken. They have been largely faithful to the intent of Congress in passing the Act. The courts have not defined "equal" work to mean "the same" work, as the House of Representatives apparently intended, but have defined it as "substantially the same" work.[10] No doubt, this enlargement was necessary if the Act was to have any application at all. On the other hand, the courts have resisted plaintiffs' arguments by eschewing a definition that would have permitted comparison of *different* jobs that are on the same *level* with respect to skill, effort, and responsibility. Thus the courts have stayed close to Congressional intent by avoiding comparable worth comparison but have adopted a "substantially equal" work standard to give the EPA some scope.

Although sensible, this solution raised the question of what to do about the "equal skill, effort, and responsibility" requirements of the statute. Again, the courts were creative, but only at the expense of language consistency. They interpreted the "equal" in this phrase, in contrast to their interpretation of "equal" in the "equal work" term, to mean "the same level as" and thereby permitted skill, effort, and responsibility comparisons of the so-called "extra" tasks that differentiate two jobs that are otherwise the

---

*Some economists would assert that wage rates themselves assess the relative productivity of workers performing different jobs. In addition to certain theoretical objections to the use of wage rates for this purpose, their use would be inappropriate under the EPA because that Act implies that some jobs which carry unequal wage rates are, in fact, equal; this could never be true if the wage is taken as a measure of the productivity of job incumbents.

same. (This interpretation is more fully explained in Chapter 5.) This has meant that a limited form of comparable worth comparison is permitted in EPA cases, a fact that has, nonetheless, failed to appease feminists who prefer a broader court interpretation of "equal work."

The import of this discussion of the statute's language is to show that the language is unclear, forcing the courts to make unguided judgments about its meaning and ultimately forcing them to give contradictory meanings to the key term "equal." The result has been decisions that are inconsistent, contradictory in their outcomes for the litigating parties, and frequently defensible only as subjective and arbitrary judgments.

Other Aspects of Equal Work

The major issue in most EPA cases is whether two jobs, one held by women, the other by men, are equal. The case fails unless this is established, no matter how large the wage differential between the jobs or how similar the jobs appear to be with respect to their "worth" to the employer.

Equal work can be established only through job comparisons. Individual or sex group comparison either of skills possessed or of job performances are irrelevant to this threshold question. Rather, the comparisons must be of job tasks.

How similar must the tasks of two jobs be in order for the jobs to be considered equal under the law? This question has been faced by the courts in nearly all EPA cases, yet no satisfactory answer has evolved. In enacting the law, Congress apparently thought that most cases under it would involve men and women who were doing the same or nearly the same work. But men and women are rarely found doing the same work, thus prosecutions under the Act quickly became involved with jobs that were similar but not the same.

If the courts had interpreted "equal" to mean "same," adjudication would have been greatly simplified, but then the application of the Act would have been extremely limited and employers would have been able to evade it through very small differentiations of job tasks. Thus, "equal" was authoritatively defined to mean "substantially" equal in the 1970 *Wheaton Glass* case, and since then the courts have struggled to apply that standard.[11]

The importance of subjectivity in applying the standard is quite apparent. Even when a court assesses job equality quantitatively—for example, the percentage of work time that employees of two job classifications perform common tasks—the translation of "substantial" into quantitative terms must be somewhat arbitrary. Under a quantitative criterion most people would agree that if two jobs have 95 percent of their work time in common they are substantially equal. But with only 75 percent commonality, the evaluation might be different.

In Chapter 5 I will deal with this and related issues in greater detail, arguing that the courts need to pay more attention to the essentiality of the tasks which are not common to two jobs, regardless of the proportion of work time they consume. Even where a particular task is rarely performed, if the capacity to perform it is essential and this capacity commands a wage premium in the labor market, a job that requires it is not equal to one that does not.

Equal Work Criteria

In judging whether two jobs are equal under the statute, the first step is to determine that there exists a substantial core of job tasks common to both jobs. Since this common core is found in most cases, job equality issues tend to focus on the noncommon or "extra" duties of the jobs being compared. The four statutory criteria used for evaluating the extra duties are skill, effort, responsibility and working conditions. The first three must be "equal" to establish the equality of two jobs. Working conditions need only be "similar."

"Skill" refers to capacities that are obtained through experience, training, schooling, and ability, according to the Department of Labor's *Interpretive Bulletin*.[12] To be relevant for job comparisons, skill must be used on the job, not merely possessed by job incumbents or cited on job descriptions as helpful but not essential for job performance.

"Effort" is the physical or mental exertion used in the performance of a job. Comparison of the effort used in two jobs can be difficult when there is variation in some job tasks. Further complicating the analysis are possible sex differences in the amount of effort required to perform a particular task. If a male job requires the lifting of 30-pound boxes and a female job only 20-pound boxes, it is not clear that men exert more effort than women, due to sexual differences in strength. EPA cases have not made this distinction explicitly, perhaps because of the necessarily arbitrary judgment it would entail. Tacit judgments of this type, however, may have underlain some court findings of job equality despite heavy lifting duties performed by men.

"Responsibility" refers to the range and magnitude of accountability associated with a job.[13] It is sometimes assessed with respect to the consequences of an error in job performance. If the error would be quickly discovered or would involve little loss to the employer, job responsibility can be said to be slight.[14]

The "similar working conditions" requisite for equal work has been interpreted technically by the courts (including the Supreme Court) to include just two elements: surroundings, for example, the existence of toxic chemicals or fumes; and hazards, the probability and possible seriousness of injury. The courts have concluded that working conditions and the other equal work criteria were added to the Act by Congress in direct response to pleas from industry representatives to make commonly used job evaluation factors the bases for determining job equality.[15] According to testimony on the equal work bill presented to Congressional committees in 1963, industrial definitions of the "working conditions" factor in job evaluations included only "surroundings" and "hazards."[16] The Supreme Court's acceptance of these industrial definitions in *Corning Glass* has meant that "working conditions" cannot be interpreted in common sense terms. More importantly, this means that day and night are not different working conditions. Day and night jobs that are otherwise equal are equal under the statute.

The Court took a "term of art" or technical approach to its interpretation of "working conditions."[17] Since "skill, effort, and responsibility" are also job evaluation factors having technical definitions, consistency requires that these terms also receive technical interpretations by the courts. Such consistency has not yet developed and may not occur. The great danger in a technical approach to defining these terms and to determining job equality is that job evaluation is not an exact science, by any means, and definitions of job factors and elements are not universal among different job evaluation systems.

THE PLAINTIFF'S CASE

The structure of a plaintiff's case can be broken down into four elements. The plaintiff must show that (1) within an establishment (2) employees of the opposite sex (3) are receiving unequal pay (4) for work that is equal.* Having previously discussed the most crucial fourth element, I will briefly outline the other three.

Establishment

In general, an "establishment" is synonymous with a business location; although in some circumstances each plant or facility in a particular location can be considered an establishment, while in other circumstances, especially central administratin, physical facilities which are in different locations can all be considered one establishment. Using the establishment concept in the EPA ordinarily limits violations to one business location; unequal pay for equal work performed in separately located plants of a multiplant firm is lawful.

---

*For greater detail see Charles A. Sullivan, "The Equal Pay Act of 1963: Making and Breaking a Prima Facie Case," *Arkansas Law Review* 31 (1978): 545

The important point, then, is that the establishment reference leaves untouched unequal pay for equal work when the work is performed for separate employers. As noted in Chapter 1, it is not a violation of the Act for employer A to pay women 50 cents an hour less than employer B next door pays men for the same work. Of course, if this job allocation of workers by sex is produced by hiring discrimination (on the part of either employer), the much more comprehensive antidiscrimination statute, Title VII of the Civil Rights Act, would apply.

Employees of the Opposite Sex

It is clear from the historical concern which motivated the EPA that the law was aimed at situations where men and women worked at the same job for unequal pay in close proximity with each other, and at situations where men and women were segregated into two job classifications that actually encompassed equal work but were compensated unequally. The law, however, was not written with sufficient precision to confine it to these two sets of circumstances. Furthermore, these circumstances of sexual wage discrimination in employment are not frequently found, in part because they are not desirable ways for employers to operate, as previously discussed, and in part because rigid sexual segregation among jobs has been reduced since 1963, by Title VII among other things. There exists at least token employment of women in nearly all occupations these days.* Consequently, applying the EPA to employees who are paid "at a rate less than the rate at which the (employer) pays wages to employees of the opposite sex" is not a simple matter.

One question is whether the law applies to individuals, two department managers of the opposite sex, for example. Congressman Goodell, in the House debate on the measure that became law, stated that the bill had been changed during subcommittee deliberations to refer to "employees" rather than "employee," in order to avoid prosecution of isolated cases of wage discrimination.[18] That view has been ignored by the courts, however, and some equal pay cases do involve job and pay comparisons between individual men and women.

A more complex issue is whether the law applies to women in a lower paid job who claim their work is equal to that of a higher paid job that

---

*For evidence of female movement into nontraditional jobs, see Beatrice G. Reubens and Edwin P. Reubens, "Women Workers, Nontraditional Occupations and Full Employment," in American Women Workers in a Full Employment Economy, U.S. Congress, Joint Economic Committee (1977), pp. 103–26. For evidence that, in the aggregate, female employment remains highly concentrated in traditionally female occupations, see Barbara B. Reagan, "De Facto Job Segregation," in the same volume, pp. 90–102.

employs both men and women. Further, does the Act apply when both the lower and higher paid jobs employ both sexes? In such circumstances do both the lower paid women and lower paid men have EPA claims?

In certain fact situations, the courts have answered all these questions affirmatively, yet the law on these matters is not settled. If authoritative affirmative answers were established, it would mean that wage differentials among jobs could be widely challenged, even where an employer has provided equal job opportunity for women. In Chapter 8 I will argue that where equal job access exists, EPA violations should not be found unless there is clear evidence that the equal access is perfunctory, designed to conceal an employer's wage discrimination against women.

UNEQUAL PAY

If there are differences in the wage rates paid to men and women, their pay is unequal. This criterion has been used for the vast majority of actions under the law. Differences in most other forms of compensation can also demonstrate unequal pay. Certain issues in the latter area have not yet been decided; their importance, however, is likely to be limited for most applications of the Act.*

Exceptions to the Equal Pay Requirement

An employer rebuttal of an EPA *prima facie* case—one that establishes the presumption of equal work for two jobs, subject to refutation—can, of course, attack each of the points made by the plaintiffs, particularly the issue of equal work in the jobs compared. The employer can also offer an affirmative defense for a wage differential, that is, evidence and argument that the differential has a nonsexual basis.

The law provides four exceptions to the requirement that equal wages must be paid for equal work. A wage differential for equal work is lawful if it is based upon a seniority system, a merit system, an incentive system, or "any other factor other than sex."

If a wage differential for equal work is to be considered an exception to the equal pay requirement under any of the first three factors, the employer must have established a practice of systematically using the factor as a basis of wage differentiation. For example, greater length of service for men than women will not justify a higher wage for the former when equal work exists,

---

*City of Los Angeles, Department of Water and Power v. Manhart, 435 U.S. 702 (1978) involved pension compensation for men and women. The case was filed under Title VII, but was decided under EPA standards.

unless seniority is widely and consistently used as a pay basis for other members of the employer's work force. A system which is both informal and unwritten can qualify, but its terms must have been communicated to affected employees.[19]

It is not clear whether a wage-differentiating factor which falls into the fourth, catch-all category must also be systematically applied to employees. In part, this category may have been established to include pay differences which are obviously equitable even though not systematically based. For example, a wage difference between a male engineer with twenty years of seniority and a female engineer with five would be viewed by almost everyone as equitable and, consequently, is probably lawful under the Act even though the employer does not consistently base pay progression on seniority. Similarly, evidence of substantial differences in job performance would be a basis for a wage difference under the catch-all category even where no standard system for paying according to merit has been established. The equity of pay for performance is so well accepted that a system for implementing this principle need not exist if clear performance differences between two employees doing equal work can be established. Pay differentiation based upon differences in sales, output, or some other incentive can be viewed comparably.

Seniority and incentive systems that base pay on quantity of output are widely accepted as equitable and easy to administer bases for pay differentials. Thus, their application to EPA cases is relatively simple. Merit is also widely accepted as equitable in theory—most people believe that better performance should be rewarded with better pay—but practice is another matter. It is difficult to assess performance on jobs that do not have a measurable output, and can influence such assessments. Consequently, at least one writer would require employers who plead merit system defense for a sexual wage differential to show that the system is gender neutral in its impact, or that its disparate impact on women is justified by business needs.[20] While merit systems in principle are gender neutral, it is not at all clear how those that in practice are not can be shown to be justified by business need. The business necessity of job hiring tests can be demonstrated for Title VII purposes by the correlation between test scores and measures of job performance (validity); however, merit reviews are very difficult to validate in this fashion because they are assessments of job performance, and alternative measures of job performance against which the validity of the merit reviews can be assessed are usually not available.

The question here is whether employer assessments of the individual performance of employees should be disregarded as a basis for wage differentials because the employer's average assessment of female employees is lower than that of male employees, and because the employer can offer no proof of the validity of his or her judgment. The fact is that much of business success depends upon the quality of employer or management judgments that cannot be validated at the time they are made. If enough of these judgments are sound, the business will probably prosper. Judgment of employee performance is fundamental to the successful operation of a business and most other kinds of organizations. If, as a matter of public policy, we wish to encourage the development and growth of business enterprise, employers must be permitted to make these judgments. And they should not be considered discriminatory unless they are shown to be so, either by their intent or by their inconsistency with whatever facts about employee performance plaintiffs can assemble.

Catch-all Exception

The general exception to the equal pay requirement, "any other factor other than sex," could include a vast number of factors associated with pay. In practice, however, seniority, merit review, and incentive systems are the principal elements that differentiate the pay of individuals on like jobs. Thus, the number of "other factors" likely to be introduced as affirmative defenses is rather limited.

It is interesting to note that education, the variable most favored by economists for explaining wage differences, is not obviously a factor other than sex that can justify a wage differential. The government's interpretive manual suggests that greater schooling is a defense for unequal pay only when the schooling is required for performance of the higher paid job.[21] Nonetheless, some courts have given excessive deference to schooling per se, by crediting it as a statutory basis for unequal pay.[22]

Training programs designed to provide experience and learning that are likely to be helpful for advanced positions are a legitimate basis for unequal pay so long as the programs are open to both sexes. Greater "economic benefits" from male workers than from female also fall into the catch-all category; however, the identification of such benefits is difficult. In the one case where an employer was able to establish the legitimacy of the "economic benefit" exception, *Hodgson v. Robert Hall Inc.,* it was shown that the average salesman produced a greater dollar volume of sales and profits than did the average saleswoman.[23] This case may have little precedent value, however, for reasons that will be discussed in Chapter 6. I simply note here that if, in *Robert Hall,* the salesmen sold more expensive clothing than the saleswomen, this means they had more responsibility, and a finding of unequal work under the "responsibility" cirterion of the statute would have been justified. In that case, the question of economic benefit would not have arisen.*

---

*The reader is forewarned that the courts have considered the notion of economic benefit or

In summary, if the plaintiff makes out a *prima facie* case of equal work in an equal pay case, and if the defendant is unable to rebut that evidence or is unable to show that the wage differential falls under one of the Act's exceptions to the requirements of equal pay, the defendant loses the case.

---

value in two different ways. First, they have examined differential economic benefit as a defense for higher pay to men, as in *Robert Hall*. Second, they have used economic benefit as a criterion for deciding whether women and men are doing equal work, as in *Shultz v. Wheaton Glass* (421 F2d 259, CA 3, 1970) and *Hodgson v. Brookhaven General Hospital* (436 F2d 719, CA 5, 1970). Thus, Chapters 4 and 5 treat economic benefit in connection with equal work judgments, while Chapter 6 examines it as a defense for unequal pay.

NOTES

1. 29 U. S. Code, 206 (d).

2. Henry C. Black, *Black's Law Dictionary*, 5th Ed. (St. Paul, Minn.: West Publ. Co., 1979), p. 480.

3. David Belcher, *Compensation Administration* (Englewood Clifs, N.J.: Prentice-Hall, 1974).

4. *U. S. Cong. Rec.*, 109, 9197 (May 23, 1963).

5. Ibid., 9196.

6. Ibid., 9193.

7. Ibid., 9209.

8. "Equal Pay for Equal Work," *Economic Journal* 59 (1949): 384–98.

9. *Wirtz v. Midwest Manufacturing Corp.*, 58 LC 32070 (S.D. Ill. 1968); 29 *U.S. Code of Fed. Reg.*, 800.151 (1982).

10. *Shultz v. Wheaton Glass*, 421 F2d 259 (CA 3 1970).

11. Ibid.

12. 29 *U.S. Code of Fed. Reg.*, 800.125 (1982).

13. Ibid.

14. Elliott Jacques, *Equitable Payment* (New York: Wiley, 1961).

15. *Corning Glass Works v. Brennan*, 417 U.S. 188 (1974).

16. U.S. Senate, Subcommittee on Labor and Public Welfare, 88th Cong., 1st Sess., *Hearings: Equal Pay Act of 1963*, 99.

17. *Corning Glass Works v. Brennan*, 417 U.S. 188, 201 (1974).

18. *U.S. Cong. Rec.* 109, 9208 (1963). See also, Charles A. Sullivan, "The Equal Pay Act of 1963: Making and Breaking a Prima Facie Case," *Arkansas Law Review* 31 (1978): 545.

19. 29 *U.S. Code of Fed. Reg.*, 800.144 (1982).

20. Sullivan, op. cit., p. 589.

21. 29 *U.S. Code of Fed. Reg.*, 800.125 (1982).

22. *Wirtz v. Citizens First National Bank*, 58 LC 32050 (E.D. Tex. 1968); *Neeley v. American Fidelity Assurance Co.*, 17 FEP 482 (W.D. Ok. 1978).

23. 473 F2d 589 (CA 3 1973).

4

THREE EPA CASES

EPA cases fall into two general categories. One involves individual plaintiffs, for example, a woman who has succeeded a man as a department head, or a woman dispatcher who alleges that she is doing work equal to that of her co-dispatcher, a male. Many of these cases are idiosyncratic and, consequently, do little for the general cause of female pay equity, although they occasionally help to establish legal principles, for example, that a woman cannot be paid less than a man simply because she will accept a lower salary.[1]

The second category of cases involves groups of employees: women who are employed in one job classification and men who are employed in a second, higher paid class. These group cases are considerably more important to the remedial purpose of the EPA because they can affect employers' job classification and wage structures. In particular, they can influence employer (and union) decisions to consider certain jobs as "women's work" and to pay less for the performance of these jobs than if they are not so considered.

This chapter critiques three important cases which fall into the second category. The cases are examined in some detail in order that the reader may perceive the full flavor and context of the employment situations that have been affected by the Act. Since the plaintiffs prevailed in all three cases, the pay practices of certain employers had to be changed. The fact that these plaintiffs won their cases should not be misconstrued, however; plaintiffs, whether the government or individuals, appear to lose considerably more EPA cases than they win because of the difficulty of proving equal work. The cases presented here, *Shultz v. American Can Company—Dixie Products, Shultz v. Wheaton Glass* and *Corning Glass v. Brennan*, are among the most frequently cited of all EPA cases. *Corning Glass* is the only EPA case to have been decided by the U.S. Supreme Court.

SHULTZ V. AMERICAN CAN COMPANY
—DIXIE PRODUCTS

At the time of this trial in 1968,[2] the Dixie Products Division of the American Can Company, manufactured paper containers at its plant in Fort Smith, Arkansas. Over 500 employees worked in the manufacture and distribution of these products, with production employees represented by the Pulp, Sulphite, and Paper Mill Workers Union. The effective date of the EPA was June 11, 1965, for American Can since the Act provided that, where a collective bargaining agreement existed at the date of the law's enactment, the law would become effective upon the termination of the agreement or two years from the date of enactment, whichever came first. Up until this time, collective bargaining agreements between American Can and the union provided separate male and female wage rates for all job classifications that employed both sexes. On the effective date of the Act, sex differentials, per se, were eliminated and all jobs were opened to both sexes.

The jobs in question here were (1) "cup machine operator, a.m. and p.m. shifts" and (2) "cup machine operator, night shift." The former, which employed 60 to 65 women, encompassed two shifts: 7:00 a.m. to 3:00 p.m. and 3:00 p.m. to 11:00 p.m. The night shift classification employed approximately 25 men from 11:00 p.m. until 7:00 a.m. There was no difference between job classifications in the operation of the cup-making machines; all shifts used the same machines. The only job difference was that the night shift operators loaded the machines with paper, while on the day shifts this function was performed by utility men or maintenance personnel. The rolls and blanks of paper, loaded by hand and equipment, weighed from 50 to 1500 pounds, depending on the requirements of each machine. Night shift operators spent 2–7 percent of their work time on the loading operations. The wage differentials and sexual segregation between the day and night shifts had existed at least since the early 1950s. In June 1965, day operators were paid $1.85 an hour and night shift operators were paid $1.96. The latter also received a night shift premium of 10 cents an hour.

Despite the opening of all jobs to both sexes in June 1965, no women had worked as night shift operators by the time of trial. One woman had applied by mistake for a night shift vacancy but withdrew her bid when she realized the opening was on the night shift. Another woman had submitted a bid on a night opening, but she was a probationary employee, and the collective bargaining agreement prohibited bids from probationary employees. Apparently, no other bids from women had been submitted. The effective collective bargaining agreement provided that employees who bid on the job of night shift operator were given forty-five days to demonstrate that they could perform all duties of the job. This provision was directed to performance of the loading operations since all other duties of the day and night shifts were the same.

The trial court decided this case for American Can, principally on the grounds that the loading task of the night operators made the jobs unequal.[3] It seems likely that the opinion of the court was influenced by the fact that no eligible women had applied for the night position, although the opinion does not explicitly connect this fact with its finding of inequality between the two operator jobs.

The trial court was reversed at the circuit level. The most important reasons given by the higher court for its reversal were: (1) the loading functions of the night operators were "minor and incidental" rather than "substantial"; (2) no wage differential existed among night shift operators, even though there were differences in the amount of time they spent on the loading tasks; (3) the paper-handling tasks on the day shifts were performed by unskilled workers who were paid less than the female operators of those shifts; and (4) the initial establishment of the wage differential was based partly on sex.

I believe that all of these reasons involve judgmental error and, therefore, do not support a finding of equality between the night and day shift positions. Beyond that conclusion, the circuit court's reasoning, even if considered sound, demonstrates the difficulty of reaching decisions on the equality of two jobs. An analysis of the circuit decision is presented here; additional assessments are integrated into subsequent chapters.

First, in concluding that the 2–7 percent of work hours that the night operators spent on handling and loading paper was insignificant, the court emphasized quantitative significance and ignored substantive significance, namely the essentiality of the paper-loading function. No matter how little time a particular task requires, if its performance is essential and a wage premium must be paid to hire people to perform it, it is significant for equal work comparisons.

Second, because the performance of a particular work task is the basis for a wage difference between two jobs does not mean that variation in effort among those who perform the task must be accompanied by corresponding wage variation. Job classifications nearly always encompass positions that vary somewhat in tasks and the amount of time given to each. If all members of a particular job class perform a task not performed by any member of another class, the two job classes are unequal even if the amount of time spent on the differentiating task varies among those who do it. In other words, it is reasonable for an employer to group jobs into classifications based on the general commonality of tasks performed, and it is reasonable to pay one wage rate for all jobs in a classification, rather than a variety of wage rates based on slight differences in the time spent on any particular task. Small variations in the use of that capacity do not affect its price (wage). Work that requires this capacity is not equal to work that does not, and this should be recognized in work comparisons under the EPA.

Third, the fact that the workers who did the paper handling and loading on the day shifts were paid less than the operators (female) on those shifts is irrelevant to the question of whether the day and night operator positions were equal. This question requires comparing operator jobs that did not require paper loading with those that did. What was paid to employees who did only the loading work is statutorily irrelevant. The low pay received by these employees does not prove that the effort of operators who did and did not perform this function was equal.

Fourth, there was a basis only in a very restricted sense for the court's conclusion that the origins of the wage difference between day and night operators was sexual. When American Can set up its 11:00 p.m. to 7:00 a.m. shift, it no doubt presumed that few women would want to work those hours and that a premium over day-shift wages would have to be paid to attract men to the night shift. An advantage of employing men, however, was that they could perform the loading task without help from utility personnel. Thus, the higher wage was established to attract workers to a night shift and with the rationale that performance of the loading task deserved extra pay. The only sense in which the wage differential was sexual was that the firm excluded women from applying for the night shift, based on the assumption that they would be unable to perform the loading function. Hiring practices, then, not the day-night wage differential, were sexually biased. The higher wage was needed to staff the night shift. (American Can paid a small shift differential to its night operators in addition to a higher basic rate. The shift differential should be viewed as pay for the inconvenience of working the night shift; that is, it would have existed had both day and night operators been male. The higher basic rate for night operators was necessary to attract the kinds of employees who would work at night—principally men, in the company's judgment). The company decided that a higher wage would be required to attract night operators, that this higher wage would attract qualified male workers, and that, consequently, the loading function could be added to the night job. These were all reasonable decisions, untainted with sexual discrimination. (The refusal to hire women for night work was sex discrimination, however.)

In contrast, the alternatives permitted by the EPA are inefficient, if not unreasonable. First, prior to the effective date of the Act, American Can could have paid night-shift operators the same wage it paid day-shift operators, but since most workers do not like to work the "graveyard" shift, the number and quality of workers who could have been hired for that shift would probably have been inadequate. Second, the day-shift wage could have been raised to the level required to attract high quality operators to the night shift. That solution would, of course, raise the firm's labor costs and make the day position more attractive for most workers than the night position. Either solution has a cost imposed by the Act.

Another part of the circuit opinion requires comment. The court wrote that an EPA violation was not cured in 1965 when the company opened the night shift to women.[4] This is certainly true, for once the court decided that the jobs of the day and night shifts were equal, the law calls for an equalization of pay, not equal access. However, the court failed to address the issue of whether the absence of any female bidders for the higher paid night-shift job, following the opening of this job to women in June 1965, was evidence of the inequality of the day- and night-shift jobs. If the jobs were equal, women could be expected to bid for the night job because of its higher wage rate. The absence of bids despite the pay premium would seem to have indicated that the night job was less desirable than the day one and that the two jobs were unequal, in EPA terms, due to the greater effort or less desirable working conditions associated with the night operator position. Since judgments about job equality by courts far removed from the day-to-day industrial scene are fraught with difficulty and the standards for such judgments inadequate, it is unfortunate that the circuit court in *American Can* ignored a simple empirical test of the equality of two jobs. The test—job bids by women for the better paid job—is a good one because it is based upon the behavior of people who should know well the similarities and differences of the two jobs being compared. (This test will be discussed again in Chapter 7.)

In sum, the court reasoned unsoundly to reach the conclusion that American Can's day and night shift operator jobs were equal, and it ignored strong evidence that they were not. One may surmise that the court was unduly influenced by the company's past record of discrimination against women in the hiring process.

SHULTZ V. WHEATON GLASS COMPANY

The 1970 Wheaton Glass case authoritatively established the "substantially equal" standard for judging equal work in EPA cases.[5] It is useful to examine the case in some detail to better understand the court's difficulties in applying the law.

The Wheaton Glass Company is a large manufacturer of glass containers that employed 2,200 production employees at the time this case was tried in 1968. The operation in quesion involved the inspection and packaging of glass bottles manufactured in the company's plant. This job was performed by "selector-packers" who picked glass containers by hand from a conveyor belt, visually inspected them, and packed those accepted into adjacent cardboard cartson. In late 1967, 230 of the selector-packers were women, employed at $2.14 an hour; 276 were males, employed at $2.35 an hour. The males had sixteen additional duties not required of females according to the trial court's opinion. The additional duties included lifting of cartons in excess of 35 pounds, mechanical adjustments to equipment, and other miscellaneous tasks. A company engineer studied the selector-packer jobs for two weeks in the fall of 1967 and concluded that the women spent 98 percent of their working time on the primary duties of selecting and packing, while the men were similarly engaged for 82 percent of their time, the balance of which was given to the additional duties. On the average, each man lifted 200 cartons in excess of 35 pounds each week.

The differentiation of male and female jobs began in 1956. Until then all selector-packers had been male. A shortage of males in the local labor market (rural New Jersey) caused the company to recruit females for the first time, but only after an agreement was made with the Glass Bottle Blowers Union, which represented production employees, that females were to be confined to light duty work, not including the lifting of cartons weighing over 35 pounds. In addition, females were not to displace males, but could be hired for vacancies created by male attrition. The union and company also agreed to a wage rate for females which was 10 percent below that paid to males. The company reverted to hiring only males from 1962–1966 because the limitations on the duties of females hindered the efficiency of selector-packer operations and because males were once more available in the local labor market. In mid-1966, however, labor market conditions again required the hiring of women.

In bringing this case, the U.S. Department of Labor alleged that the male and female selector-packers performed equal work and that the occasional performance of additional tasks by males was merely incidental to the total job cycle and did not make the male and female jobs unequal. The district court judge rejected these contentions, finding instead that Wheaton had proven the jobs to be unequal by showing that "men are required to exert additional effort, to possess additional skill, and to have additional responsibility."[6]

This conclusion appears to be reasonable, based upon the evidence presented in a sixteen-day trial. Although the trial court's opinion is not entirely clear, the principal evidence behind the court's conclusion appears to have been the large number of additional duties performed by the male selector-packers and the company evidence that 18 percent of the men's time was spent on these additional duties. The company (and union) in this case appeared to have created a new, light job out of the old one and to have set a lower wage for it based on management's view that women could do the light job and would do it at a lower wage than that being paid to men for the same job with its heavier work.

This bifurcated job structure, and the associated segregation of women in the lower paid position and men in the higher paid one, appears to have been discriminatory under Title VII of the Civil Rights Act because of the attendant implications of refusal to hire women for the heavy job and men for the light one. It is by no means evident, however, that the job structure itself amounted to an EPA violation of unequal pay for equal work. The increased job specialization which Wheaton created simply emulated the conduct of business firms which has existed at least since the Industrial Revolution. This specialization has produced and continues to produce economic benefits in the form of lower production costs. Those benefits cannot justify violation of Title VII in the form of hiring discrimination. On the other hand, this kind of job specialization, where certain components of one job are made into a new, distinct job, does not constitute an EPA violation merely because men perform the more general work and women the more specialized.

The trial court's decision to this effect was appealed by the Department of Labor to the Third Circuit Court of Appeals, which reversed the lower court and found the company was violating the EPA. The most important reasons given by the court for its reversal were the following: (1) contrary to the district court judgment, the DOL did prove that the male and female jobs were equal; (2) the additional duties performed by male selector-packers were also carried out by thirty-seven "snap-up" boys, who did these heavy duties exclusively and were paid only $2.16 an hour for doing so, just 2 cents more than the rate paid females; (3) the motive for the creation of two jobs from the original single one "clearly appears to have been to keep women in a subordinate role. . .and to emphasize the subordination by both the 10 percent differential between male and female selector-packers and the 2 cents difference between snap-up boys and female selector-packers.'" These findings of fact and reasoning do not, in my judgment, support the conclusion that Wheaton was violating the EPA.

The circuit court's conclusion that there was "no adequate support either in findings of fact or in the record" for the district court's judgment that the male and female jobs at Wheaton were unequal is inexplicable. The senior court acknowledged the evidence submitted by the company that male selector-packers spent an average of approximately 18 percent of their total time on work proscribed to women. Apparently, however, it rejected the probative value of that evidence, for it stated that the district court had not found the submitted evidence to be factual. But this is simply nit-picking. It is evident that the district court did credit the company evidence on this point, because its opinion described the method employed by the company to arrive at the 18 percent figure, as well as the result itself. The circuit court stated further that the trial court had made no finding that *all* male selector-packers performed any or *all* of the additional tasks. This, again, is a quibbling rationalization of the court's judgment. The district court judgment was clearly based on findings that significant additional duties were part of the job of the male selector-packer and that they were performed regularly by job incumbents, whether or not all men performed all of the sixteen additional tasks. As in *American Can*, what made the male and female jobs different and unequal in *Wheaton Glass* is that the male job required the *capacity* to perform the extra duties and this capacity had to be paid for, regardless of variation in its actual use by job incumbents. In these nearly capricious explanations, the circuit court appears to be grasping for justifications of its reversal of the trial court.

The second basis for reversing the Wheaton trial court was also faulty. The circuit court, having noted the wage rates of $2.14 for female selector-packers, $2.16 for snap-up boys (who performed only lifting and like duties), and $2.35 for male selector-packers, concluded that there was "no rational explanation why men who at times perform working paying 2 cents per hour more than their female counterparts should for that reason receive 21-1/2 cents per hour more than females for the work they do in common."[*] The court on this basis held that the extra duties performed by the male selector-packers had no "economic value" that justified a higher wage than that paid to female selector-packers.

The principal problem with this reasoning, stated previously with respect to *American Can*, is that it does not pertain to the language of the Act. That language requires proof that the female job is equal to the male job; the duties of and pay for a third, associated job are not relevant to this primary comparison. Furthermore, the court's logic is wrong. There could easily be a rational reason why the additional duties that were the basis for the $2.35 wage paid to male selector-packers were compensated at only $2.16 when performed by snap-up boys. For example, Wheaton may have considered the position of snap-up boy to be relatively unimportant, both quantitatively (only thirty-seven were employed) and qualitatively, and therefore may have established low hiring qualifications for it in terms of age, experience, reliability, and commitment to long job tenure. The male selector-packer job, on the other hand, required the performance of physical tasks in combination with inspection and packaging duties, and therefore required different qualifications than the position of snap-up boy. How to set a price on the combination of qualities required for male selector-packer work cannot be deduced from the wage rate paid to persons who perform a small component of that work (whether one relies on the market to determine wages or some system of job evaluation). Wheaton and the Glass Blowers Union had decided to pay one rate for its employees who performed only inspector-packing work, another rate for those who performed only lifting and related physical work, and a third, higher rate for those who performed both. The court erred in concluding that this arrangement was irrational and consequently in finding that Wheaton had violated the statute. The court should have first reached a conclusion, based on statutory criteria, about the equality of the male and female jobs. If it had found them to be equal, the court then might have concluded that the wage structure was irrational as well as discriminatory.

Finally, the circuit court's conclusion that Wheaton's original motive for bifurcating the selector-packer job was to keep women in a subordinate role appears to be wrong. The company created the female job (with the Union's acquiescence) in order to tap a new source of labor. The new job was circumscribed in its duties because the union wanted to maintain job security for men, because the company probably believed that few women were capable of heavy lifting, and because the circumscribed duties provided a visible justification for attaching a lower rate to it. (The market might have supplied females for the full selector-packer job at a wage below that being paid males; however, the union would not permit such an undercutting of its wage, and Wheaton may have recognized the obvious problem that can arise when females are being paid less than males for the same work.) It seems clear that the motive for creating the new job at a lower wage was business efficiency—to obtain labor at a low cost. The motive would have been the same had the new labor supply been teenagers, blacks, the handicapped, or retired persons. Presumably, Wheaton felt that women were the best and most numerous new workers available at the time.*

Whether Wheaton also wished to subordinate women because it believed that, in the nature of things, women should be subordinate cannot be determined. Since a purely business motive was well served by the company's actions, it is doubtful that an insidious discriminatory motive, whether present or not, played a significant part in the job specialization Wheaton created. There can be no doubt that the apparent refusal of Wheaton to hire women for the higher paid inspector-packer job was discriminatory under Title VII. (The court opinions do not indicate whether women ever sought the higher paid job or men the lower paid one.) While Wheaton's restructuring of the selector-packer job made economic sense, because it provided a higher wage for the more physical work for which it had relatively few job applicants and a lower wage to the less physical work for which it had plenty of applicants, restricting the more physical work to males and the less physical to females was not just. Removal of the sexually

---

*Black workers, however, would have been able to perform the physical work included in the full selector-packer position. If the circumscribed job had been offered to black workers, it would have been obvious that the circumscription was for the purpose of paying a lower wage rate. With women, it was possible for Wheaton to claim that the circumscription of job duties was based on a (debatable) judgment that they could not perform the heavy lifting. The lower wage was then rationalized as due to the circumscribed duties.

based restrictions on job access would have made the job arrangements just, as well as economically sensible.

The segregation of men and women into separate jobs appears to have troubled the court in Wheaton, as it has troubled many courts in EPA cases. The court seemed to believe that the unwillingness of the company to permit "willing and able" women to perform the inspector-packer job that required heavy lifting was indicative of discriminatory intent. That conclusion is, no doubt, correct, but the form of discrimination practiced—job segregation—was a violation of Title VII rather than the EPA. Refusal to hire women for certain jobs is hiring discrimination, not wage discrimination. The court's comment implies that, had females been employed in the full (male) selector-packer position, an EPA violation might not have been found. But there is no language in the EPA that suggests that a violation of the Act depends upon job segregation. The law is directed to job comparisons, not the allocation of men and women among jobs. Furthermore, equalizing job opportunities for men and women is not a permissible remedy for an EPA violation, because the statute makes increasing the female wage to the male level the only permissible remedy. Perhaps what went through the minds of the third circuit judges in Wheaton, and has gone through the minds of other judges in other EPA cases, is that the elimination of job segregation *should* be the solution to alleged EPA violations even if it is not the solution specified by law. Judges, faced with EPA charges that require them to make difficult decisions as to whether certain jobs are substantially equal, may well come to believe that a better resolution of the EPA charges would be the opening of all jobs to men and women alike. If women had equal access to the higher as well as lower paid jobs the wage differential between them would be less important than where equal access does not exist, and the wage differential would probably not be attributed to sex. Given the complexities of EPA job comparisons, it is little wonder that many of the decisions appear to turn on the matter of job segregation, the elimination of which is seen by many people as the most fundamental need of women workers. This matter will be discussed further in Chapter 7.

Not only did the Wheaton decision fail to make sense under the EPA and in economic terms, it was also particularly ironic because it contradicted an illustrative example, given during the House discussion of the bill in 1963, which was designed to show Congressional intent for the Act. The Wheaton case turned out to be an almost perfect replication of an example that had been presented by floor manager Goodell, during the 1963 consideration of the bill, to show expressly the intent of Congress in enacting the legislature. Congressman Goodell stated:

A difference in pay between male selectors and packers and female selectors and packers would be valid if, in addition to the duties performed by the female selectors and packers, the male selectors and packers are required to lift the crates off of the assembly line, or sweep up the room or work on the load dock during slack periods.[9]

The *Wheaton* decision, dealing with these exact circumstances of selector-packers, obviously conflicted directly with Congressional intent for the EPA, at least as expressed by a key sponsor of the legislation. The conflict occurred because the EPA could not have been applied to the industrial world without at least some expansion of the Congressional intent that existed at the time of its passage.

CORNING GLASS V. BRENNAN

The only EPA case decided by the U.S. Supreme Court was *Corning Glass v. Brennan*.[10] This followed a split between the second and third circuits in two very similar cases decided in 1973, both involving Corning Glass manufacturing plants. The Supreme Court's decision, as well as the lower court decisions, dealt principally with a narrow semantic question. The statute requires, as one of the criteria for equal work, that two jobs be performed under "similar working conditions." The issue in *Corning Glass* was whether night work, as opposed to day work, is a working condition under the statute.

The average person would immediately respond that night work is most definitely a working condition, generally an undesirable one. The Supreme Court, however, decided otherwise, using a technical definition of the statutory term. The case is informative because it illustrates the difficulty of wage regulation through the legislative and judicial processes.

Facts

One of the Corning suits filed by the Department of Labor involved the firm's plant in Corning, New York, the other its plant in Wellsboro, Pennsylvania; otherwise, the facts of the two cases were very similar. Corning began night shifts in certain of its glass manufacturing operations around 1925 and hired inspectors for those shifts. Previously it had employed day inspectors, all of whom were women. In 1925 however, New York law prohibited the employment of women between 10:00 p.m. and 6:00 a.m., and Pennsylvania law prohibited it between midnight and 6:00 a.m. Consequently, Corning was forced to recruit men for its night shift. It recruited them from its male day employees and had to pay these men a wage equal to that which they had been receiving for various day jobs in order to get them to transfer to the night shift. The net result was that the male night inspectors were paid 53 cents an hour, while the female day inspectors were paid 24 to 28 cents an hour. This situation persisted until the effective date of the EPA, except during World War II, when women inspectors were employed at night and were paid the same wage rate as men. The relative size of the night-day differential fell considerably over the years. In 1925, it was 104 to 121 percent; in 1966, the maximum absolute differential was 22.5 cents an hour, approximately 10 percent above the wage then received by female inspectors.[11]

Pennsylvania law was changed in 1947 to permit night employment of women where public transportation was available or where the employer provided transportation. Public transportation was not available in Wellsboro, and Corning considered it economically infeasible to provide transportation for female night employees. In 1953, New York permitted the employment of women over 21 on factory night shifts where the Industrial Commissioner found satisfactory transport and safety conditions and granted approval. Apparently, Corning never sought such approval.

The American Flint Glass Worker's Union organized Corning's plants in 1941 and negotiated a night shift differential of 5 cents an hour for all night shift jobs. The existing wage base differential between day and night inspectors was left intact, however.

When the EPA became effective June 11, 1964, Corning had separate, plant-wide male and female rate schedules. It then merged these schedules to eliminate lower rates for females; however, the historical difference between day and night inspectors was continued by assigning the day inspectors to a lower wage classification than the night inspectors. In June 1966, Corning opened the night inspector jobs to women, permitting them to use their plant seniority to bid for vacancies and to "bump" onto the night shift during workforce reductions. Well over half of the night inspector vacancies during the next four years were filled by women.[12] Turnover of night inspectors was "substantial"[13]; the Wellsboro plant had 45 night inspector jobs and turnover produced 395 openings for them between October 1966 and June 1970.[14]

Trial Court Decisions

The trial court in the Pennsylvania *Corning* case decided in favor of Corning on the ground that night work made the working conditions of the day and night inspectors dissimilar; in other words, night work fell under the "working conditions" term of the statute, and the day and night positions were not equal because nighttime is a different working condition from daytime.[15]

The New York court, on the other hand, decided that the night and day jobs were equal and that the wage difference between them violated the

Act.[16] It did not deal expressly with whether time of day was a working condition under the statute, but the two jobs could not have been found equal if it were. Thus, by implication, the New York court held that nighttime was not a working condition. Interestingly, the court's finding of equal work was based on the fact that Corning's own job evaluation system gave equal point ratings to the two inspector jobs.* The Company's argument that its job evaluation system did not consider time of day worked—because it is a wage factor rather than a job evaluation factor—was considered, but the court, obliquely, found that Corning's general night shift differential "adequately compensates employees for working undesirable times of day."[17] The court apparently did not realize that it needed to decide the threshold question of whether time of day worked is a working condition under the statute, before considering the significance of general night shift wage differential.**

Circuit Court Decisions

Upon appeal, both circuits faced the similar working conditions requirement head on and reached opposite conclusions, the second circuit deciding that time of day worked was not encompassed by this phrase and the third circuit deciding that it was.[18] The court interpretations of the "working conditions" term were crucial for their respective decisions. Once the third circuit decided that the term encompassed time of day worked, the working conditions of the night and day inspector positions were obviously dissimilar and unequal under the statute. On the other hand, after the second circuit decided the jobs were equal, because "working conditions" did not encompass time of day worked, Corning still had a chance to show that the wage differential between them was based on a non-sexual factor—the inconvenience of night work. This defense actually had no chance, however; it was used up, so to speak, by the general night shift differential paid to all night shift employees. Corning could not successfully agrue that night shift inspectors should be paid another wage premium on top of the

---

*The Pennsylvania court also used the firm's job evaluations to decide that the two inspector jobs were equal aside from time of day worked. This conclusion was made ambiguous, however, by the court's "supplemental findings of fact" that (1) male inspectors on the steady night shift have performed additional duties requiring substantially greater physical effort, including heavy lifting and pushing, than have the same titles on the day shift"; and (2) "male inspectors on the night shift have spent 25 to 30 percent of their time doing manual labor, heavy and light." *Hodgson v. Corning Glass Works*, 341 F. Supp. 18, 23 (M.D. Pa. 1972).

**The court may have viewed Corning's working conditions argument as an affirmative defense for its wage differential, rather than what it was—an argument that the plaintiff had failed to meet its *prima facie* burden of showing equal work under the statute.

the general night shift premium they already received. Thus the interpretations of "working conditions" decided both cases.

Again ironically, the second circuit used the testimony of Corning's former Director of Industrial Relations, Ezra G. Hester, before House and Senate subcommittees that were considering the equal pay bill in 1963, to reach its decision that Congress had not intended time of day worked to be encompassed by "working conditions." Hester had testified against requiring equal pay for "equal work on jobs the performance of which requires equal skill," which was the original phrasing of the bills introduced into Congress in 1963.[19] He had contended that industry relied heavily on job evaluation systems to establish wage differentials among jobs, and that most of these systems considered effort, responsibility, and working conditions, in addition to skill. Hester had argued successfully for the inclusion of these three additional criteria as determinants of job equality under the EPA. He had explained to the subcommittees the industrial meaning of these criteria, using Corning's own job evaluation plan to do so. The Corning plan had included just two factors under working conditions: "surroundings" (requiring evaluation of the intensity, and frequency of exposure to "elements") and "hazards" (requiring evaluation of exposure to hazards, possible frequency of injury, and possible seriousness of injury).[20] Time of day worked was not mentioned.

The second circuit concluded, correctly in my judgment, that the House of Representatives had responded directly to this and similar testimony. The court quoted the report of five minority members of the Committee on Education and Labor, which had held hearings on the bill and recommended its passage:

> The concept of equal pay for jobs demanding equal skill has been expanded to require equal effort, responsibility, and similar working conditions as well. These factors are the core of all job classification systems and the basis for legitimate differences in pay.[21]

Since the inclusion of working conditions in the statute was in direct response to Hester's testimony, the court reasoned that its intended meaning was the same as that specified in the Corning job evaluation plan. Time of day worked was not part of that meaning.

The third circuit, on the other hand, was not persuaded that Congress intended to give a narrow meaning to the term "working conditions," to the extent of excluding time of day worked from that meaning. It was impressed, however, with a statement made by Congressman Goodell as he explained the EPA legislation to his fellow members on the floor of the House of Representatives. Goodell's final point of explanation was as follows:

Finally, standing as opposed to sitting, pleasantness or unpleasantness of surroundings, periodic rest periods, hours of work, difference in shift, all would
logically fall within the working condition factor.[22]

Largely on the basis of this statement, the third circuit decided that
time of day worked was a working condition under the Act and, therefore,
the two inspector jobs could not be equal. Both of the circuit courts but-
tressed their respective conclusions through analysis of the *Report of the
House Committee on Education and Labor*. This report had attempted to
clarify the meaning of the factor-other-than-sex exception to the Act by
providing examples that would fall under this exception, one of which was
time of day worked.[23] The examples were ambiguous, however, since some
were clearly illustrations of unequal work rather than of the catch-all exception to the equal pay requirement. Due to the ambiguity, it was possible for
the two circuits to read the report differently, which they did, each in support of its overall decision. The final detailed views of the two courts on the
committee report are given in an appendix to this chapter.

Supreme Court Decision

The Supreme Court by a five to three vote (Justice Stewart did not par-
ticipate in the decision), supported the second circuit's decision against
Corning. It found that the "similar working conditions" requisite for equal
work determination, and thus application of the Act, did not emcompass
time of day worked. The working conditions requirement, the Court said,
was adopted by Congress "in direct response" to pleas from industry
representatives for an expanded definition of equal work.

Indeed, the most telling evidence of Congressional intent is the fact that the
Act's amended definition of equal work incorporated the specific language of
the job evaluation plan described at the hearings by Corning's own representative—that is, the concept of "skill," "effort," "responsibility," and
"working conditions."[24]

The reader is reminded that Corning included only work "hazards"
and "surroundings" as parts of its working conditions factor. Thus, Corning's attempt to have the courts declare its day and night shift jobs unequal
failed, largely because Corning's own representative had testified eleven
years earlier that the working conditions criterion for equal pay, which he
was urging Congress to adopt, did not include time of day worked. Without
Hester's testimony, it is likely that Congressman Goodell's statement—that
difference in shifts would render two jobs unequal for EPA purposes—would have been viewed as authoritative.

The *Corning* decisions illustrate the difficulties of attempting to deal with sex discrimination through a focus on wage rates. Corning was certainly guilty of sex discrimination because of its refusal (before 1966) to hire women for its night inspector job; this was a violation of Title VII. Whether its wage structure for the night and day positions was also sexually discriminatory is not so clear. The firm provided a higher base wage for its night inspectors because of its beliefs that males were needed for this position and that a higher wage was required to hire males. Thus the higher night wage was economically based; it was required by the greater market wage of men. The intent of the higher wage was not to discriminate against women but to attract men to the night position.

Nevertheless, the higher wage for male inspectors was inextricably linked to sex through the labor market; it existed only because men rather than women were employed as night inspectors. Consequently, it violated the EPA; the Act does not permit an establishment to pay a higher wage for men because their market wage is higher than that of women. The EPA was aimed at remedying this market difference.

The Supreme Court could see that Corning's wage premium for its night inspectors was sex-based. Unfortunately, to find that the firm had violated the Act, the court had to give a peculiar meaning to the widely used term "working conditions." If it had not given a narrow, "term of art" meaning to "working conditions," that term would have encompassed time of day worked, and the two jobs would have been found to have different working conditions and to be unequal. The court's definition of "working conditions" was peculiar because nearly everyone, from job applicants to collective bargaining participants, considers time of day worked to be a working condition. The court's explanation that when "Congress has used technical words or terms of art 'it [is] proper to explain them by reference to the art or science to which they [are] appropriate,' "[25] is unpersuasive. In this regard, the court gave excessive weight to Hester's testimony during the 1963 Congressional hearings, as shown by its conclusion that the EPA incorporated ". . .the well-defined and well-accepted principles of job evaluation. . . ."[26] With respect to wage setting generally, it is at least a mild exaggeration to say that job evaluation principles are both well-defined and well-accepted.

Although it is true that most job evaluation plans do not consider time of day worked under the "working conditions" factors (because it is seen as a differentiation of pay rather than work tasks), much variety exists among these plans. Some do not include a working conditions factor at all, and others use this factor to encompass numerous elements of the work environment.[27] More importantly, the wages and salaries of most American workers are not administered under a system of job factor evaluations.[28] Thus the term of art definition given to working conditions by the Supreme Court is not widely used; on the other hand, a broad definition of that term, to include time of day worked, is recognized by practically all workers, employers, and unions.

In sum, the Supreme Court in *Corning Glass* was forced to endorse a false and intuitively strange meaning of "working conditions" in order to find the male and female jobs equal and to find that Corning had violated the EPA. It is doubtful that such a procedure enhances public confidence in the Act or in antidiscrimination statutes generally.

A better approach to the kind of sex discrimination exhibited in *Corning* would be to focus, not on wage setting, but on job access. Corning was clearly guilty of job discrimination against women. An appropriate remedy for that discrimination would have been to open the night inspector job to women (in addition, of course, to providing them back pay for the wage difference between the day and night jobs) and to let the relative supply of all workers to the day and night positions determine the wage differential. If a job discrimination claim had been filed under Title VII, presumably this outcome would have obtained.

It is less clear that Corning also discriminated against women with respect to their wages. Only if sex discrimination encompasses wage differences resulting from the payment of market wages to men and women was Corning's behavior discriminatory in a wage sense. Even accepting this debatable definition of discrimination, as does EPA law,[29] the *Corning* decisions illustrate the difficulty of identifying and proving its existence. In this instance a nonsensical definition of working conditions, and thus of equal work, was required.

The Remedy

The Supreme Court also supported the second circuit's judgment that Corning continued to be in violation of the Act after it opened the night shift to women (and the day shift to men) in 1966. The court concluded that, once Corning had been found in violation of the EPA, it could remedy its violation only by equalizing the pay of its day and night inspectors (except for the general night shift premium). The statute states clearly that, where it has been violated, the wage for the lower paid job must be raised to the level of the higher paid job.

The wage equalization remedy, forced by the language of the EPA, provided an immediate wage increase (plus back pay) to Corning's day inspectors, most of whom were women. One can only guess at the secondary effects of this remedy. The wage increase was permanent unless, during subsequent collective bargaining, Corning and the Glass Blowers Union negotiated smaller increases for the inspector position than for other jobs. Since the statutory wage increase raised labor costs and presumably increased the available supply of day inspectors, reasons for reducing the relative wage of inspectors did exist. The higher wage that Corning was required to pay day inspectors could have resulted in reducing their employment, or in substituting some men for women if the former had any cost or productivity advantages. The clearest secondary effect of the wage equalization would have been an increase in the attractiveness of the day inspector job relative to the night position. The employee turnover facts cited indicated that the night job was not very attractive even when it carried a higher base wage than the day position.

Without empirical research, observations about the effects of the wage equalization must be speculative. Consequently, one cannot compare it with the open access remedy that would have prevailed had Corning been found guilty of job discrimination against women under Title VII. (I am purposely neglecting the back pay remedies under both statutes.) What can be said is that, in terms of regulation, the EPA remedy went beyond the open access remedy that Corning had adopted and that would have been required by a Title VII job discrimination charge. The EPA forced wage equalization for the day and night inspector jobs, rather than merely giving men and women equal access to them. How one compares the consequent gain for day inspectors, most of whom were women, with the reduced freedom for wage determination that also resulted from the EPA is not at all clear.

APPENDIX:

Interpretation of the *Report of the House of Representatives Committee on Education and Labor*

The second and third courts of appeal differed in their interpretations of the following paragraph of the House committee report:

Three specific exceptions and one broad exception are also listed [in the bill]. It is the intent of this committee that any discrimination based upon any of these exceptions shall be exempted from the operation of the statute. As it is impossible to list each and every exception, the broad general exclusion has been also included. Thus, among other things, shift differentials, based on *time of day worked*, hours of work, lifting or moving heavy objects, differences based on experience, training, or ability would be excluded. . . . [emphasis added][33]

The second circuit read this paragraph to mean that time of day worked came under the broad exemption of the Act for "differentials based on any other factor other than sex." It apparently translated the "thus" that begins the last sentence to mean that because the broad general exclusion had been written into the statute, time of day worked, among other things, would be a legitimate basis for a wage differential. Under this conclusion, time of day worked became a possible justification for a wage differential and not a part of the similar working conditions criterion, which was one of the requisites for applying the Act.

This interpretation by the second circuit seems reasonable, but so does the subsequent contrary interpretation by the third circuit. That court concluded that the House of Representatives report quoted above does not provide the basis for concluding that time of day worked can unambiguously be construed to fall under the general exemption of the statute. This is because some of the other examples listed in the last sentence of the quoted paragraph definitely do not come under the general exemption but, rather, are requisites for a finding of equal work and the application of the statute. The court cited "lifting or moving heavy objects" as examples of "effort" and "experience, training, or ability" as examples of "skill." Equal "effort" and "skill" are both requisites for application of the Act. Since the paragraph lists examples of elements which would clearly make the Act inapplicable, along with time of day worked, the third circuit held that it could not unambiguously conclude that the latter fell under the general exemption to the equal pay requirement.

Which of the circuit courts correctly interpreted the quoted paragraph from the House report depends upon the way the issue is posed. The second circuit appears to be correct in response to the issue framed as follows: is time of day worked as used in the committee report an example of requisite "working conditions" or an example of a factor other than sex upon which a wage differential can be legitimately based? "Thus" in the quoted paragraph suggests that the draftsperson intended the subsequent elements to be examples of the "broad general exclusion" (any factor other than sex) cited in the immediately preceding sentence. If so, then the listing of examples of the requisite criteria for *application of the statute* following the "thus," along with "time of day worked" and other examples of the general exclusion, was probably a mistake, created because the draftsperson was understandably confused as to the difference between job conditions which would make the Act inapplicable and conditions which would justify a wage differential between the sexes.

On the other hand, the question may be put another way: is "time of day worked" as used in the committee report unambiguously an example of either the requisite "working conditions" criterion or of the factor-other-than-sex exemption? The third circuit's answer is correct. That court found that the intended meaning of the "time of day worked" example in the committee's report was ambiguous, and it went on to decide the time of day issue on another ground.

NOTES

1. *Futran v. RING Radio Co.*, 24 EPD 3140 (N.D. Ge. 1980).

2. 424 F2d 356 (CA 8 1970).

3. *Wirtz v. American Can Co.*, 58 LC 32071 (W.D. Ark. 1968).

4. *Shultz v. American Can Co.*, 424 F2d 356, 359 (CA 8 1970).

5. *Shultz v. Wheaton Glass Co.*, 421 F2d 259 (CA 3 1970).

6. *Wirtz v. Wheaton Glass Co.*, 57 LC 32040, 43410 (D.C. N.J. 1968).

7. *Shultz v. Wheaton Glass Co.*, 421 F2d 259, 264 (CA 3 1970).

8. Ibid., 263.

9. *U.S. Cong. Rec.*, 109, pt. 7: 9209 (May 23, 1963).

10. *Corning Glass v. Brennan*, 417 U.S. 188 (1974).

11. *Brennan v. Corning Glass Works*, 480 F2d 1254, 1256 (CA 3 1973). The Court opinions in this litigation do not provide the 1966 wage rates. I have estimated them from the 1964 wage rates provided in *Shultz v. Corning Glass Works,* 319 F. Supp. 1161, 1166 (W.D. N.Y. 1970).

12. *Hodgson v. Corning Glass Works*, 474 F2d 226, 230 (CA 2 1973).

13. Ibid.

14. 480 F2d 1254, 1257 (CA3, 1973).

15. *Hodgson v. Corning Glass Works*, 341 F. Supp. 18 (M.D. Pa. 1972).

16. *Shultz v. Corning Glass Works*, 319 F. Supp. 1161 (W.D. N.Y. 1970).

17. 319 F. Supp. 1161, 1169.

18. *Hodgson v. Corning Glass Works*, 474 F2d 226 (CA 2 1973); *Brennan v. Corning Glass Works*, 480 F2d 1254 (CA 3 1973).

19. U.S. Senate, Subcommittee on Labor, Committee on Labor and Public Welfare, *Hearings: Equal Pay Act of 1963*, 88th Cong., 1st Sess., (1963) pp. 96–104.

20. Ibid., p. 99.

21. U.S. House of Representatives, Committee on Education and Labor, 88th Cong., 1st Sess., *Report No. 309,* (1963), p. 8.

22. *U.S. Cong. Rec.*, 109: 9209 (May 23, 1963).

23. *Report No. 309,* op. cit.

24. *Corning Glass Works v. Brennan*, 417 U.S. 188, 201 (1974).

25. Ibid., 201. The court is here quoting from *Greenleaf v. Goodrich*, 101 U.S. 278, 284 (1880).

26. Ibid.

27. Thomas H. Patten, Jr., *Pay: Employee Compensation and Incentive Plans* (New York: Free Press, 1977), pp. 234–235; Howard Risher, "Job Evaluation: Mystical or Statistical," *Personnel* 55 (1978):25.

28. Donald J. Trieman, *Job Evaluation: An Analytic Review* (Washington, D.C.: National Academy of Sciences, 1979) pp. 49–50; Gary Craver, "Survey of Job Evaluation Practices in State and County Governments," *Public Personnel Management* 6 (1977):124.

29. For example, *Hodgson v. Brookhaven General Hospital*, 436 F2d 719, 726 (CA 5 1970).

30. U.S. House of Representatives, *Report No. 309,* op. cit.

5

EQUAL WORK STANDARDS

The essence of most EPA cases is whether women in a lower paid job class are doing work equal to that performed by men in a higher paid class. If the court decides that the two jobs do indeed entail equal work, the pay for the lower paid job must be made equal to that of the higher one unless the employer can establish that the existing pay differential is based upon seniority, merit, an incentive system, or some other nonsexual factor. Since the existence of one or more of these statutory exceptions to the equal pay requirement can frequently be determined by straightforward facts, the much more subjective determination of the equality of work content is usually the crucial matter in EPA cases.

The most important issues under equal work assessments can be grouped as follows: (1) job content vs. equal skill, effort, and responsibility, (2) the meaning of "substantial" equality, and (3) the weight given to job evaluation evidence.

JOB CONTENT V. EQUAL SKILL, EFFORT, AND RESPONSIBILITY

It was pointed out in Chapter 3 that the language of the EPA is ambiguous for establishing standards to determine the equality or inequality of any two jobs. When the fundamental "equal work" phrase is interpreted in accordance with the legislative history of the Act to mean substantially the same work, the addition of the "equal skill, effort, and responsibility" criteria for defining equal work becomes redundant. Jobs which have substantially the same task content necessarily have equal skill, effort, and responsibility; there is no need to make this obvious fact explicit. On the other hand, the legislative history of the Act precludes an interpretation of its definitional language that would make sense, both syntactical and otherwise: that equal work is work on the same level with respect to skill, effort, and responsibility and on a similar level with respect to working conditions.

Faced with the ambiguities of the statute's definitional language, and precluded by its legislative history from a comparable-worth interpretation that would have made that language logically consistent, the courts have creatively dealt with the construction problem, although they have not well articulated their solution. They have developed a two-pronged standard for deciding whether two jobs are equal. First, they have interpreted the "equal work" phrase to mean that the jobs being compared must have a common core of work tasks.[1] Second, they have applied the "equal skill, effort, and responsibility" criteria to the work tasks which differ between two jobs—the extra duties, so to speak—and "equal" in this application is taken to mean equivalent rather than the same. Thus to be equal, two jobs must first have a substantial common core of work tasks, and secondly, they must require equivalent skill, effort, and responsibility for the work tasks they do not have in common.

This interpretation is paradoxical in the sense that "equal work" is construed to mean substantially the same work, while "equal skill," etc., is construed to mean equivalent or the same level of skill, etc. Nevertheless, this interpretation appears to be the only way to make sense out of both the ambiguous phrasing and legislative history of the law. To avoid the complexities of job comparisons, the courts might well wish they could ignore the comparable-worth criteria of "equal skill, effort, and responsibility" and "similar working conditions," and decide the equality of jobs simply on the basis of whether the common core of overlapping work tasks is large enough to show substantial equality. These criteria are in the Act, however, and to their credit, the courts have applied them but have limited their application to the comparison of the non-common work duties of two jobs.

One of the results of this statutory construction is that comparable-worth theory—the view that wage discrimination claims can be based on unequal pay for jobs requiring comparable (equivalent) qualifications—is applied in EPA cases. The application is very slight, however, since it is limited to jobs that have a great deal of work content in common.

The two-step standard for job equality was not clearly formulated until 1977 when the third circuit decided *Angelo v. Bacharach Instrument Company*,[2] thirteen years after the effective date of the law. Even in this case its articulation is partially implicit. Angelo had employed a well-known industrial engineer, Bertram Gottlieb, to evaluate certain light assembly (female) and heavy assembly (male) jobs. Gottlieb asserted at trial that the light and heavy assembly jobs were substantially equal based upon his evaluations of various components of the skill, effort, responsibility, and working conditions criteria. These job evaluations had produced similar point totals for the two sets of jobs. The court rejected this testimony, however, on the grounds that it failed to establish the equality of *job content*.

> The Equal Pay Act comprehends a threshold requirement, evident in the legislative history and confirmed in the case law, that the jobs to be equated be substantially the same. The requirement of equality of job content inheres in the statutory term, "equal work."[3]

The court pointed out that Gottlieb's job evaluations—although showing the equality of the two job classes when the points assigned to each evaluation factor were totaled and also showing the equality for the two jobs of *each* of the skill, effort, responsibility, and working conditions factors—actually disclosed the statutory inequality of the jobs. For example, Gottlieb had concluded that the two jobs required equal effort because the greater mental-visual effort on one was offset by the greater physical effort of the other. Thus, effort on the two jobs was equal only because two different kinds of effort balanced out. But the statute requires the *same* effort over at least a common core of job duties. Therefore, by showing that the effort factors in the two jobs were different, though equivalent, Gottlieb's evaluations actually demonstrated statutory inequality.

The plaintiff's error in *Angelo* was in attempting to apply the comparability standard to the entire work content of the two jobs. A comparability standard would have been acceptable for the nonshared tasks of the two jobs. The court wrote in this regard

> . . .mental effort might perhaps be weighted against physical effort to show the insignificance of incidental differences between two positions having substantially the same primary content.[4]

The failure to expand upon this statement may indicate the court's lack of awareness that it was, in effect, articulating a two-step focus for determining job equality—the primary core of common tasks, and the noncommon extra duties—and applying comparable worth standards to the second step. Regardless, the court's opinion did delineate the two-step procedure, although with much greater detail on the first step of establishing the core of common content. *Angelo* merely made more overt the procedure that many courts had been following in EPA cases—consideration of the equality of the skill, effort, and responsibility required for two jobs, but only in connection with the different work tasks of those jobs.

By stating that a common core of the same work content was the first requisite for equal work, this third circuit opinion, rejected a comparable worth interpretation of the Act that would have been possible through job evaluation evidence of equal point totals for skill, effort, responsibility, and working conditions. Without the prerequisite of a common core of equal work content, the language of the EPA might well be interpreted to embrace the job evaluation meaning of equality: equal point totals regardless of whether the skill, effort, responsibility, and working conditions are substantially the same or are merely comparable in terms of evaluation points. The decision in *Angelo* prevented a broadening of the equal pay standard to jobs that appear to require similar levels of skill and other factors. It is difficult to see how any other decision could have been reached because of the legislative history of the statute.

Nonetheless, because of the ambiguities of the statute, the two-step procedure for assessing job equality was not always followed before *Angelo* and may still not be observed by some courts. In a 1972 case, the fourth circuit stated that the Secretary of Labor did not have to show that three women employees performed work identical to that of a male employee; ". . .rather, he must show that what they did required equal skill, effort, and responsibility."[5] This statement appears to overlook the threshold requirement of showing substantial equality of job content and to suggest, instead, that the work of the women was equal to that of the men if equivalent skill, effort, and responsibility were required, regardless of the commonality of job content.*

The court's subsequent analysis of the two jobs was consistent with these interpretations. The analysis focused on the comparability of the qualifications required by the male position's extra duties, and it did not consider their quantitative or other importance relative to the common work content of the male and female positions. If the latter had been considered, the content of the two jobs may have been found not to be substantially equal, in which case, inquiry into the comparability of the qualifications required for the extra duties of the male if would have been irrelevant.

Some courts may have been led to overlook the threshold requirement of substantial equality of job content by the oft-cited fifth circuit decision in *Hodgson v. Brookhaven General Hospital.*[6] That decision set out certain rules for analyzing extra duties of a higher paid job. It also rather obliquely implied that, to be considered equal, jobs must "entail most of the same duties,"[7] but if failed to develop that phrase into any kind of operational standard for assessing the equality of job content. Consequently, some courts may have been influenced to judge work equality by examining the

---

*A more or less similar statement was made by the court in *Hodgson v. Daisy Manufacturing Company*, 317 F. Supp. 538, 541 (W.D. Ark. 1970), yet the subsequent analysis dealt with the differences between the male and female jobs, after a substantial core of tasks common to both had been shown. It appears that the courts often cite the "equal skill, effort, and responsibility" requirements loosely, so that their application to the total content of jobs is suggested, but then go on to apply them only to the noncommon duties of two jobs.

nature of the extra duties of the higher paid job, as long as *some* commonality of the two jobs was present.

Differing interpretations of this matter apparently continue into the 1980s. The ninth circuit recently stated that the plaintiff's burden of proof (in addition to that of showing wage inequality) was to show that "the work of employees of one sex required the exercise of substantially equal skill, effort, and responsibility and was performed under working conditions similar to that of employees of the opposite sex."[8] If the court's omission of the equal job content threshold requirement was not simply inadvertent, this statement appears to unwarrantably broaden the reach of the equal pay standard.

THE SUBSTANTIAL EQUALITY OF WORK

Once the courts decided that an equal pay claim did not have to show the absolute identity of two jobs being compared, they were faced with the task of comparing jobs which differed in minor, but not necessarily unimportant, content and deciding whether they met the "substantially equal" test. The decisions made under this standard do not, collectively, comprise a clear body of law. Rather, they appear to be arbitrary and inconsistent, creating a situation of considerable uncertainty.

One could argue, based on the legislative history of the Act, that the courts should not be making these kinds of decisions because Congress intended the Act to apply only to nearly identical jobs. However, only if the equal work standard had been statutorily restricted to "completely identical" jobs could the courts have avoided difficult decisions about job equality. Any departure from that absolute standard requires close scrutiny of job duties and requirements and requires judgments as to their degree of equality. After almost two decades of litigation, it is evident that there are only arbitrary answers to the question of how similar jobs must be to be considered "substantially equal" for EPA purposes.

Shultz v. Wheaton Glass[9] authoritatively provided the principle that two jobs need be only "substantially equal" to come under the Act. *Hodgson v. Brookhaven General Hospital*[10] further codified this principle by stating that two jobs are not equal if one of them (1) involves additional tasks which (2) consume a significant amount of time of all those receiving the higher pay and (3) have economic value commensurate with the pay differential.[11]

These principles fail to provide satisfactory standards for judging job equality. First, they do not indicate what is to be considered "a significant amount of time" that, when spent on extra duties, makes a job unequal to the comparison job. It could be one hour a week for certain skilled extra duties, while ten hours a week might not be significant in other instances. Perhaps a precise standard would be useful, even though it would be necessarily arbitrary. For example, it would be helpful to have a rule that two jobs cannot be considered equal unless at least 75 percent of the work time of both sets of incumbents is spent on work tasks that are common to both jobs.

Second, the Brookhaven rule that all members of the higher paid job class must perform the extra duties is unreasonable, as I have noted previously, because the work content of a job class is not constant over time, nor is it necessarily the same for all incumbents of the class.

Third, the criterion that *Brookhaven* stated for evaluating the extra duties, "economic value," while not included in the statute, could be useful because the basis for payment of wages is economic value. However, this concept needs more development than the court provided if it is to be applied sensibly. Determining the economic value of extra effort (the criterion intensively examined by the *Brookhaven* court) is a difficult task, as shown by the tortured analysis of *Shultz v. Wheaton Glass*, the authority cited by *Brookhaven* for its economic value criterion. More will be said on this subject below.

The court in *Brookhaven* attempted to supplement the statutory requirements for assessing the extra duties required on one job but not the other to which the first was being compared. The language of the Act indicates that extra duties make two jobs unequal only if they entail greater skill, effort, and responsibility and working conditions dissimilar to the comparison job. The court added the criteria of time, universality, and economic value to try to assist assessments of the significance of the extra duties. While this effort is understandable in view of the difficulty of making job comparisons, the criteria added have not helped to produce persuasive EPA decisions.

Under the principles established by *Brookhaven*, courts have decided that heavy lifting which took up only 2-7 percent of male work time did not make the lifting job unequal to a similar job that did not involve lifting.[12] Neither did the extra duties of hospital orderlies, involving one or two catheterizations each week,[13] or even two or three each day,[14] make their jobs unequal to otherwise similar positions of hospital aides. Janitors who filled a pop machine for 15-20 minutes a day, emptied garbage cans for 35-40 minutes twice a day, operated a floor stripping machine, and removed snow were found to have jobs substantially equal to those of maids who did none of these tasks except remove garbage on occasion.[15]

The last case, particularly, illustrates the question raised by these decisions generally. South Davis Community Hospital employed nine maids and three janitors—one janitor during the day, one at night, and one for relief work. If the maid and janitor jobs were in fact equal, as the court found, why was the hospital employing janitors and paying them more money than maids? Why didn't the hospital employ only maids and thereby reduce its wage costs? It would appear from the court's decision that the hospital management was either incompetent or derived some discriminatory satisfaction out of hiring male janitors and paying them more than was necessary to get its janitorial functions carried out.

It is likely that neither of these apparent explanations accurately describes the hospital's reasons for paying janitors and maids differently. Instead, it is more likely that the hospital established the janitor classification because it required physical effort not required by the maid position and that the greater physical effort had to be paid for. In other words, the greater physical effort had a greater economic value. Persons who possessed physical strength and were willing to use it had to be hired, and this could be done only at a wage greater than that paid to maids. At the higher wage, males were available and were hired; the court opinion did not indicate whether women applicants were also available for the janitor position and were discriminated against in hiring.

Indeed the economic rationale for a wage difference between two jobs was made explicit in *Brennan v. Prince William Hospital*.[16] Prior to 1969, the hospital had paid aides (females) and orderlies (males) the same wage but had experienced difficulty in hiring orderlies even though only a small number were employed. Consequently, the wage for orderlies was raised to a level 10–12 cents an hour above that of aides, and orderlies were assigned the additional duty of catheterizing male patients. The fourth circuit's decision that the aides and orderlies were performing equal work, despite the occasional catheterizations done by the latter, required that the wage scale for the hospital's thirty-four aides be raised to the wage for its four orderlies. In short, the court required the hospital to pay more than was necessary to hire aides. It refused to let the hospital conform to the labor market by paying aides and orderlies the respective wages necessary to attract a sufficient number of each. The hospital's pre-1969 history indicated that it had no desire to pay orderlies more than aides. It did so only because it had to pay more to get the functions assigned to orderlies performed. The court's decision does not make economic sense; it required an above-market wage to thirty-four employees simply because the hospital paid a market wage to four other employees. The court's decision did not recognize that the characteristics necessary to perform the extra duties of orderlies had an economic value; they commanded a higher market price than did the characteristics necessary to carry out the job of aide. The court dismissed the extra duties performed by orderlies—catheterization of male patients, heavy lifting, and the provision of a physical presence to assist if necessary in restraining violent patients—as not affecting the substantial equality of the two jobs. This conclusion may have been justified by the *Brookhaven* rule requiring that extra duties consume a significant amount of time, but it is doubtful that it was justified under the statutory criteria of equal skill, effort, and responsibility. Regardless, the hospital's experience showed that the extra duties were significant in the marketplace: the market required a higher wage for their performance.

Time Required for Extra Duties

The courts often err when they judge the importance of extra duties for job equality in terms of the time required to perform these duties. First, all such decisions are necessarily arbitrary because there is no objective standard associating time and substantiality. More important, regardless of the time spent on extra duties, a substantial difference exists between two jobs when one requires characteristics in its incumbents that command a higher market wage than the characteristics of incumbents in the other job—in other words, when the employer must pay more to get one of the jobs done. Application of this economic principle would provide a much improved norm for court decisions about job equality.

One decision that recognized this principle is *Usery v. St. John Valley Security Home*.[17] Here, the district court found that nurse aides (females) did not perform work equal to that of ambulance attendants (males), even though less than 2 percent of the attendant's duties involved ambulance work and their other duties were the same as those of the aides. The court noted that the ambulance attendants were required to have training in first aid and emergency medical treatment and that these skills had to be "in readiness" regardless of the amount of their use.

The specific skills involved in the *St. John* case made their essentiality quite clear, but even where the skill or effort is more general, such as the ability to lift heavy weights, the principle is the same. If those who can and will lift heavy weights command a market wage premium over workers with otherwise comparable qualifications, employers must pay it to get their lifting done, regardless of how frequently the weight-lifting ability is used on the job. Where two jobs are the same except for heavy lifting, the position that does not require it is probably not equal to the one that does, whether the lifting is done frequently or only occasionally. This is a reasonable presumption for judicial examination of extra duties because it is based on the economic principle that employers do not pay more than is necessary to get work performed. Therefore, if a job requires extra effort, and it is paid for, the extra effort must have economic significance or value. That presumption could be overturned, of course, by a showing that the market does not require a wage premium for heavy lifting or that the premium arose from an intent to discriminate.

Separate Pay for Extra Duties

Some courts have recognized that lifting or other extra duties are a legitimate basis for a wage premium, but they have reasoned that when the extra duties are performed only occasionally, the premium should be paid only for the time spent on them and not for the total work time. In *Hodgson v. Daisy Manufacturing Company*, the court held that the employer

> . . .could, if it chose to do so, pay male paint tenders a higher rate for the small amount of working time they spend in buffing operations, and pay the men and women the same wage rate when they are performing essentially the same work.[18]

In this instance the court was correct because the paint tenders were semiskilled workers with no special skills who could readily be assigned to other semiskilled operations including buffing. However, when special skills or worker characteristics must be hired, they must be paid the going wage for them even if they are used for only a portion of work time.

In *Wirtz v. Basic Incorporated*, the district court found that a male laboratory analyst was entitled to a higher rate of pay than two female analysts while he worked the night shift, but a higher basic wage for all hours of work paid to the male than to the females was prohibited.[19] This finding followed a conclusion by the court that it was reasonable to assign night work exclusively to males where the mining, milling, and refining operations were located in "a mining community, population 769, in a fairly remote, mountainous area," and where "a very great preponderance" of workers were men.[20]

Since Basic needed an analyst who could be assigned to the night shift for alternating two-week periods, according to the court's own conclusion it needed a male for the position. Then the firm had to pay the market rate for a male analyst and pay him for all the time he worked, not just for the night work. The court's finding of an EPA violation was justified on other grounds, but that does not detract from the point that to keep an employee whose skills or characteristics command a particular market wage, the employee must be paid the market rate even when those skills are not being fully used. The court's finding in *Basic* goes against this principle. Furthermore, the equal pay objective of the ruling can be easily evaded by paying a man an especially large wage premium to do night work.

Rule That Extra Duties Must Be Performed By All Males

Job classifications frequently encompass specific positions that do not all have the same work tasks and positions that themselves have variable duties from one day or week to the next. Furthermore, jobs that differ substantially from most other jobs in a class may be included in it for wage purposes, either because they require comparable qualifications and are performed in close proximity to the other jobs in the class, or because they are part of the same technological process, or for other reasons. In short, a particular job title that is alleged to include work equal to that performed by plaintiffs can itself include positions that are not all equal under EPA definitions.

Consequently, the *Brookhaven* rule that a job's extra duties must "consume a significant amount of time of *all* those whose pay differentials are to be justified in terms of them"[21] (emphasis added) is not statutorily justified and can produce unfortunate results if followed literally. It is not clear that *Brookhaven* intended a literal application of the rule because, while the court did use the language quoted, it went on to say that employers cannot be permitted to frustrate the purposes of the Act by "calling for extra effort. . .only from one or two male employees."[22] This view is much different from one requiring that all jobholders in the higher class must perform the extra duties to justify its higher pay.

Some courts appear to have placed great emphasis on the "all" rule. The eighth circuit, in *Shultz v. American Can Company—Dixie Products*, based its finding of job equality between day (female) and night (male) operators partially on the fact that "no wage differential exists between night shift operators (who handled heavy rolls of paper) even though they are not all required to exert identical effort."[23] Such an extremely exacting requirement placed on frequently imprecise systems of job classifications is not a reasonable basis for assessing job equality.

In contrast, *Marshall v. Building Maintenance Corporation* intelligently applied this rule.[24] The Building Maintenance Corporation employed 350 heavy duty cleaners and 400 light duty cleaners. The court found that the two jobs were not equal, and the fact that up to three of the heavy duty cleaners at any one time did perform essentially the same work as light cleaners did not cause a violation. The court held that the rule must be applied with "a measure of reasonableness." It recognized that where jobs create "a spectrum of degrees of difficulty, any line drawn between classes of workers will leave a very few workers on one side of the line with jobs slightly more difficult than, but 'substantially equal' to jobs on the other side of the line."[25] The court also cited the Department of Labor's regulation that if *some* of the men are not performing the extra duty, there may be a violation.[26] Such a rule is considerably different than one requiring all men to perform the extra duty.

Economic Benefit

This criterion for assessing extra duties was derived from *Wheaton Glass* but has been used very little[27]; the concept is difficult to apply and was used incorrectly in *Wheaton*, as described in Chapter 4.

The *Wheaton* decision reasoned that since snap-up boys were paid $2.16 an hour for their lifting work, a wage of $2.36 an hour for male inspector packers could not be justified on the grounds that they too performed lifting during part of their work time. But the $2.36 wage was based on a combination of inspector-packer plus lifting duties. The issue was not how much the lifting was worth in some abstract sense, as perhaps measured by the wage to the snap-up boys, but how much it was worth when done in combination with inspector-packer tasks. The appropriate base for that determination was the wage paid to employees who did only inspector-packing. They received $2.14 an hour. Thus it is reasonable to assume that the extra 22 cents an hour paid to the inspector-packer-lifters was a premium paid for performing the inspector-packing tasks plus the lifting. In combination with the inspector-packing tasks, the lifting duties had an additional economic value.

The courts, generally, have stayed away from this difficult concept and have simply applied the statutory criteria, attempting to judge the level of effort, skill, and responsibility found in the extra duties of the higher paid job, based on whatever evidence is available to them. This procedure is statutorily sound, but the available evidence is often murky, producing judgments that are difficult and unpersuasive. In some circumstances the concept of economic value could help clarify the evidence and consequent assessment of job equality, but only if it is properly applied.

The test of whether the skill, effort, or responsibility required to perform an extra duty has an economic value should include at least two parts, each of which could provide proof that economic value does exist: (1) Does the market require that the extra skill, etc., regardless of the extent of its use by the hiring employer, be paid for with a wage premium beyond the wage paid for the job that does not require this extra skill? (2) Is it arguably equitable to pay for the extra skill, effort, or responsibility? The latter test is justified on the grounds that it is desirable (for business reasons) for an employer to enhance employee perceptions of pay equity. If either of these two conditions exists, the extra duty has a significant economic value and equality would not exist between a job requiring the extra duty and an otherwise equal job not requiring it.

ASSESSING JOB EQUALITY
THROUGH JOB EVALUATION

Because of the inherent difficulty of assessing job equality, it is not surprising that job evaluations have occasionally been submitted to the courts in EPA cases. Job evaluation involves a systematic rating of jobs on various task-related factors, such as the skill, effort, responsibility, and working conditions criteria enumerated in the statute; consequently, its results may be relevant to assessments of work equality.

Congress, however, provided evidence that it did not intend to have the federal government or courts get into wholesale job analysis and evaluation in 1962 when it substituted "equal" for "comparable" work as the standard for equal pay in proposed EPA legislation. The "comparable" standard had been used by the National War Labor Board during World War II as the policy foundation for assessing possible pay inequities between men and women who worked on *dissimilar* jobs.[28] Adoption by Congress of the "equal" standard meant that it did not want the EPA to follow this wartime experience.*

Further evidence of Congress's antipathy toward governmental use of job evaluation to enforce the Act was provided by the 1963 House debate. During the debate Congressman Goodell made the following statements:

> We do not expect the Labor Department people to go into an establishment and attempt to rate jobs that are not equal. We do not want to hear the Department say, 'Well, they amount to the same thing,' and evaluate them so they come up to the same skill or point. We expect this to apply only to jobs that are substantially identical or equal.[29]
>
> It is not intended that the Secretary of Labor or the courts will substitute their judgment for the judgment of the employer and his experts who have established and applied a bone fide job rating system. It is not the business of the Secretary of Labor to write job evaluations or judge the merits of job evaluation systems.[30]

These statements from one of the leaders in the EPA enactment indicate Congressional opposition to both a comparable worth interpretation of the statute and governmental immersion in job rating systems. The second quoted statement, however, is rather naive with respect to EPA enforcement. Once the courts had decided that "equal" work did not mean "identical" work, comparisons of job content among jobs alleged to be equal became necessary. Where these allegations of equality were raised, determination of their merit by automatically crediting employer job rating systems would have been ineffective enforcement of the law.

Shultz v. Wheaton Glass, 421 F2d 259, 265 (CA 3 1970). Congress may have become alarmed by Secretary of Labor Arthur J. Goldberg's statement to the Senate Subcommittee on Labor in 1962 that the Department of Labor would implement the equal pay for "comparable" work legislation by comparison of work and skills through "that method of job analysis and comparison which is appropriate to a particular job situation." (U.S. Senate, Sub. on Labor, Comm. on Labor and Public Welfare, *Hearing on Equal Pay Act of 1962*, 87th Cong., 2nd sess., 1962, p. 3.)

Despite Congressman Goodell's statements, the courts have at times assessed the merits of job evaluation systems, although, to their credit, they have generally eschewed the use of formal job evaluations in EPA litigation, whether offered by the employer-defendant or the plaintiff. Instead they have relied upon descriptions of job content obtained from different sources. The latter are largely factual in nature so that, frequently, all concerned parties agree on their accuracy, whereas job evaluations involve judgment about the degree of skill, accountability, etc., that particular jobs require. As noted earlier in this chapter, descriptions of job content are also much more appropriate for establishing whether two or more jobs have a substantial common core of job content.

The latter point raises the question of whether job evaluation systems can be useful at all for assessing job equality in EPA cases. Job evaluation systems do not attempt to assess the equality of the job tasks performed in two or more jobs but rather the equality or inequality of the factors, such as skill, that are required to perform *differing* job tasks.[31] In terms of factor point totals, job evaluations can be equal for two very different jobs, and they can be highly unequal for two jobs which are identical except for one or two important tasks. In short, job evaluations focus on compensable factors that are not useful for establishing the common core of job tasks which the EPA requires.

Where a common core of tasks is established by other means, however, job evaluation, in theory, can be useful for assessing the skill, effort, responsibility, and working conditions required for the noncommon duties of two jobs. If each of the factor ratings for two comparison jobs is the same, the skill, effort, responsibility, and working conditions required for the extra duties of one of the jobs are equivalent to those required by the work tasks that are common to the two jobs. If differences in the factor ratings exist, this would mean that the extra duties of one job make it unequal to the comparison job.

The major difficulty with job evaluations used in this way is their subjectiveness; they are open both to variation in judgment and to manipulation. Assessing the degree of skill, effort, and other factors required by a job is, in the final analysis after observation is complete, a matter of judgment, and the judgments of job evaluation experts can and do differ. Admission of job evaluation testimony presents problems for courts not unlike those raised by psychiatric testimony in sanity trials, because of the subjective, nonverifiable nature of the judgments that must be made in both situations. Generally, the courts would be better off making their own judgments about equal work, based on descriptions of job tasks.

The case review that follows examines the different reactions of courts to assessment of work equality through job evaluations.

Job Evaluation Cases

Early in EPA litigation a district court rejected the comparable-worth notion that equal-factor point totals for two evaluated jobs established the equality of the jobs. This court recognized that two dissimilar jobs can have equal evaluation points and also stated that jobs must be examined on their merits, apart from any classification or evaluation system.[32]

The most extensive court judgments about the use of job evaluation in EPA cases was provided by the third circuit in *Angelo v. Bacharach*,[33] discussed earlier with reference to its establishment of the threshold requirement of a common core of job content. *Angelo* established (1) that job evaluations, because they assess compensable factors rather than work tasks, cannot be used to establish the common core content of two jobs and (2) that job evaluation point totals (the aggregate of all factor points) cannot be used to assess the extra duties required in a higher paid job. These rulings appear to restrict the use of job evaluations to EPA cases where substantial equality of job content has been independently established and to evidence of point ratings for *each* of the evaluation factors included in the system.

Evidence based on a job evaluation plan that had been implemented under rather extraordinary circumstances has been credited toward a finding of job inequality. The plan had been developed well before the EPA violation was alleged at the behest of the employee's union, had been carried out by an impartial outsider, and had been thoroughly discussed by the union and employer prior to its inclusion in the parties' collective agreement.[34] Conversely, in *Corning Glass*, the firm's own job evaluation plan was used to find equality between its day and night inspector jobs.[35] Corning's plan was particularly appropriate for this purpose. It not only showed, for the inspector positions, equality of evaluation points for all job factors but also was based on the skill, effort, responsibility, and working condition factors included in the statute. Of course, the latter was no coincidence since the statutory criteria had been recommended to Congress by Corning's director of industrial relations research prior to enactment of the Act in 1963!

The most extensive use of job evaluation by a court came in *Thompson v. Boyle*.[36] The court examined various job evaluations to find that the work of journeymen bindery workers, grade 4 (females) was equal to that of craft bookbinders (male) and that the work of journeymen bindery workers of lower grades was not equal to that of craft bookbinders. The court credited the testimony for the plaintiff of an expert in job classification and much, but not all, of the testimony for the plaintiff of industrial engineer Gottlieb. The court refused to give weight to the testimony of the defendant's expert on the grounds that his evaluation of the subject jobs, performed after two days of observation, was cursory.

The court in *Thompson* followed the ruling of *Angelo v. Bacharach* that the EPA includes a threshold requirement of substantially equal job content. This requirement was met by the testimony of the plaintiff's job classification expert. The other requirement, that in regard to any extra duties the skill, effort, responsibility, and working conditions required of the bindery workers and bookbinders be equal, was met by Gottlieb's job evaluation testimony for grade 4 of the bindery workers in comparison to the bookbinders. However, similar testimony from Gottlieb relative to other grade levels of the bindery worker job was found irrelevant to the threshold requirement of establishing equality of job content.

The court in this case correctly perceived that job evaluation, by itself, cannot establish the substantial equality of job content but can establish the equality of the factors required for the performance of two jobs. The latter is the second step of the assessment of job equality and is required only after the first has been met. Given the complex and specialized nature of the jobs involved in *Thompson*, the court may also have been correct in relying on job evaluation experts, even though its reliance required a factual finding that one of the job evaluations submitted was cursory. One wonders, however, what the court would have done had both sides submitted job evaluations that appeared to be equally competent.

The results of three different job evaluations were also received by the trial court in *Marshall v. J.C. Penney Company*,[37] but here the court gave little weight to any of them. Instead, it made its own job comparisons from descriptive evidence to conclude that many of the firm's females held positions which were equal to those of higher paid males.

Penney's own compensation (evaluation) system was found to be free from sexual bias in its design but not its application at the particular store involved in the litigation (Mentor, Ohio). The court found that under this system, equally qualified males and females were hired at different wage rates. The court did not rely upon Penney's system to judge job equality. The firm also submitted the results of job evaluations prepared by an employee of Hay Associates, perhaps the best known consulting firm in this field, but the court gave them no weight because they did not assess jobs in terms of the statutory criteria of skill, effort, responsibility, and working conditions. The plaintiff submitted a job evaluation carried out, once again, by Bertram Gottlieb, whose testimony was credited in *Thompson v. Boyle*. This time the court rejected Gottlieb's work as informal and cursory. (His methods varied considerably from those used in *Thompson*, presumably due to differences in the nature of the jobs involved.)

Although no blanket conclusion is appropriate, the court's rejection of job evaluation results and reliance upon other evidence in *Penney* seems wiser than the court's reliance upon two evaluations and rejection of a third in *Thompson*. It is easy to conceive of cases in which courts would have no rational basis for choosing between two conflicting job evaluations.

Other cases involving job evaluation have raised questions about the competency of courts to evaluate this procedure even when conflicting evaluations are not present. *Wetzel v. Liberty Mutual Insurance Company*[38] gave substantial weight to a job evaluation prepared by the plaintiff's expert to establish the equality of job qualifications required of claims representatives (women) and claims adjustors (men). Inexplicably, however, the court dismissed as "legally insignificant" the expert's conclusion that "working conditions" were somewhat more difficult for the latter than for the former. (The adjustors used their cars to examine claims in various locations; the representative handled claims from an office building.) The standard by which the court decided that the difference in working conditions did not make the jobs unequal was not disclosed.

In a district court case where the results of a Hay system evaluation were submitted, the court stated, "This system does not take into account seniority or merit wage increases or differentials based on factors other than sex and, therefore, is not evidence of a job being equal in skill, effort, and responsibility."[39] Whatever this sentence means, it fails to recognize that a virtue of job evaluation is its ability to assess the equality of skill, effort, responsibility, and other factors required for various jobs, independent of the actual qualifications of persons who happen to hold the jobs at the time of evaluation. This, of course, is fundamental to the establishment of job equality under the statute. Once job equality is established, only then is it appropriate to examine whether existing pay differentials are justified by merit or any of the other exceptions provided by the law.

In sum, with some exceptions, the courts have given little weight to job evaluation evidence of job equality or inequality. *(Thompson v. Boyle* is the chief exception.) By the *Angelo v. Bacharach* decision, the courts also appear to have greatly constrained the probative value of evaluation evidence. These are wise actions because job evaluations are necessarily subjective in nature and consequently are a very malleable form of evidence. Nonetheless, due to the difficulty of assessing job equality, the parties will occasionally turn to job evaluations for this purpose.

CONCLUSIONS

The difficulties the courts have had in deciding equal work issues is indicated in their inconsistent manner of dealing with a particular set of jobs that could be expected to be similar in work tasks for all employers. For example, a legal reference volume lists nine decisions that found equal work for aides (women) and orderlies (men) and eight that found those jobs to be unequal.[40] My own, nonexhaustive search for light and heavy custodian cases (which also included other job titles, such as maids-janitors and

6

THE MARKET AS A DEFENSE
FOR UNEQUAL WAGES

The courts have consistently rejected the market as a defense for the payment of unequal wages for equal work. Put simply, a market defense is the contention that the predominately female job, which has been shown to be equal to the predominately male job, can be filled at a lower wage than the male job; males are not available at the lower wage paid to women.

This defense for unequal pay usually arises where an employer considers one job to be for women and the other for men and believes that a higher wage is required to fill the male position. Salesmen-saleswomen and aides-orderlies are examples. The two jobs within each of these pairs have frequently been found to be equal under the statute, and employers have defended unequal pay for them on the ground that males cannot be hired at the wage paid for the female positions. Other cases have involved individual men and women hired for similar positions, either simultaneously or successively, with the woman paid less than the man.

Early in EPA litigation the courts ruled that unequal pay could not be defended on the ground that women will often work for lower wages. For example, in *Hodgson v. Brookhaven General Hospital*, the court wrote, "Thus it will not do for the hospital to press the point that it paid orderlies more because it could not get them for less."[1] This view was confirmed in *Corning Glass Works* when the Supreme Court commented on the origins of Corning's wage differential between its female and male inspectors. The court wrote that the wage differential

rose simply because men would not work at the low rates paid women inspectors, and it reflected a job market in which Corning could pay women less than men for the same work. That the company took advantage of such a situation may be understandable as a matter of economics, but its differential nevertheless became illegal once Congress enacted into law the principle of equal pay for equal work.[2]

The Court's conclusion was based upon its view of the purposes of the EPA:

> The whole purpose of the Act was to require that these depressed wages of women be raised, in part as a matter of simple justice to the employees themselves, but also as a matter of market economics, since Congress recognized as well that discrimination in wages on the basis of sex "constitutes an unfair method of competition."[3]
>
> Congress' purpose in enacting the Equal Pay Act was to remedy what was perceived to be a serious and endemic problem of employment discrimination in private industry—the fact that the wage structure of "many segments of American industry has been based on an ancient but out-moded belief that a man, because of his role in society, should be paid more than a woman even though his duties are the same." (Senate Report No. 176, 88th Congress, 1st Session, 1 (1963). The solution adopted was quite simple in principle: to require that "equal work" will be rewarded by equal wages.[4]

If these views of the purposes of the EPA are correct and the Act was directed to raising the market wages of women, Congress certainly chose a timid approach to the problem. As previously stated, the EPA touches a very small proportion of female workers, and increases in their individual wages are unlikely to have a significant impact on women's wages generally. (The fact that female earnings compared to those of men have not risen in the nearly 20 years since the passage of the Act suggests the truth of that conclusion.) The Act does not affect all the women employed in jobs for which a claim of work equal to that performed by higher paid males cannot be made. It has no impact on the vast majority of females, those who are employed as nurses, sales clerks and clerical workers, for example.

If the EPA was the "solution" to the problem of low market wages for women, it was, as the Court stated, "simple in principle," but it was also almost completely ineffective for the problem to which it was directed. Apparently Congress only wanted to alter the market wage for women where that wage was manifestly discriminatory—where women performing work substantially the same as that of men were paid less. Seen in that light, it can be suggested that Congress's purposes in passing the EPA may have been to end blatant wage discrimination against women rather than to remedy the low market rates paid to them generally.

Whatever the intent of Congress, it is unlikely to have included the market as a defense for those relatively few situations where women were found to be paid less than men for work that was statutorily equal. Application of this view to actual situations has proven to be uneven, however.

SALESPERSONS

Several cases involving clothing salespersons have dealt with market defenses for unequal pay. These jobs, perhaps more than any others, are vulnerable to the EPA because men and women salespersons do essentially the same work, they cannot be substituted for each other because of customer preferences, and saleswomen can generally be hired for a lower salary than salesmen.

In *Hodgson v. J. M. Fields, Inc.*, Fields, a discount department store, followed the policy of hiring and paying its area supervisors "at whatever rate it could get them."[5] This policy produced higher average wage rates for men than women for work the court found to be equal. This simple pay practice, followed widely by employers, was not viewed by the court as a statutorily justified basis for the existing sexual wage differentials. The court opinion did not state whether the differentials resulting from the market wage policy were purely sexual or were based on sexual differences in training, experience, and other qualifications. Presumably, the former was the case since qualification differences can justify a sexual wage differential.

In *Brennan v. City Stores*, the department store offered a market defense for wage differences between its men and women salespersons, who were segregated into male and female clothing departments. The court rejected this defense, stating that "while factors other than sex justify the employer in seeking male personnel to work in conjunction with selling and fitting male clothing, this is no excuse for hiring saleswomen and seamstresses at lesser rates simply because the market will bear it."[6] Saleswomen and seamstresses had to be paid the male wage regardless of differences in the market wage of the two sexes.

One trial court did accept a market factor as partial justification for the unequal wages of men and women's clothing department heads, when the employer stated that the higher wage of the man was based partly on "salary increases granted when competitors were attempting to hire him away. . ."[7] The court did not indicate, however, whether the competitors wanted to hire this man because of his sex or because of his qualifications. Furthermore, the court did not find the work of the male and female heads to be equal. Therefore, all defenses for the unequal pay were superfluous, and the court's conclusion about the market justification for the wage differential is of little significance.

The *Fields* and *City Stores* decisions contrast sharply with *Hodgson v. Robert Hall Inc.* (discussed briefly in Chapter 3) where the court accepted "economic benefit" to the employer as a defense for a *prima facie* violation of the Act.[8] When it was shown that Robert Hall was paying unequal wages to men and women salespersons who performed equal work, the firm argued that the wage differential came under the "any other factor other than sex" exception of the statute because the reason for the differential was the greater economic value of male salespersons. Specifically, the men's clothing department had a greater average sales volume and profit per salesperson than the women's department, and in the view of the firm, and ultimately the court, these facts justified the sexual pay differences.

The court in this case may have felt that a pay policy which based wages on the average profit per salesperson by department was equitable and within the exceptions to the equal pay requirement. On the other hand, that policy is not clearly more equitable than one of paying equal wages to the male and female sales personnel because they were doing essentially the same work. The statute itself is explicitly directed to this principle. It could also be argued that the higher profitability of men's clothing called for a higher quality salesperson. However, no evidence was presented to show that the firm's salesmen had qualifications superior to those of its saleswomen.

It is likely that all of these explanations, associated with the economic benefit defense, are only rationalizations for the actual reason that Robert Hall paid more to men than to women: it had to do so in order to hire and retain salesmen of satisfactory quality, just as Fields and City Stores had to do. The greater profitability of men's furnishings did not *require* (but did permit) Robert Hall to pay more for salesmen, and it is unlikely that the firm would have done so had the market permitted salesmen to be hired at the lower wage paid to saleswomen. The court was persuaded that the male-female wage differences were nonsexual, because Robert Hall could show that an economic benefit was associated with its unequal wages while managing to obscure the fact that the unequal wages flowed from the payment of market wages.

It was fortuitous that Robert Hall could produce records showing greater profitability per salesman than saleswomen. Otherwise, its defense for the higher male wages might have failed, just as the market defense failed for Fields and City Stores. This fortuity produced inconsistent outcomes in the three cases cited. It enabled Robert Hall to justify what in reality was a market-based sex differential, while Fields and City Stores, lacking similar records, were unable to do so.

Even within the terms of the employer's defense, the *Robert Hall* court erred by finding that the greater economic benefit provided by men was a factor other than sex. In fact, the greater economic benefit was identified not on the basis of individual sales volume and associated profits, but by sex groups—the pay practice assumed that all salesmen but no saleswomen provided it. Identification of the economic benefit by sex group means that sex was the primary factor in the wage practice. If economic benefit had been the primary factor in the firm's wage practice, one or more saleswomen could possibly have received a higher salary than some salesmen. The fact that the firm's records showed some women producing a greater sales volume than some men, even though the average sales of men exceeded those of women, should have told the court that the pay practice was based on average performance by sex group rather than on economic benefit provided by each salesperson.[9]

THE MARKET AND JOB QUALIFICATIONS

While unequal wages cannot be justified by the fact that some labor markets allow employing women at a lower wage than similarly qualified men, they can be statutorily defended, under the factor-other-than-sex exception, when they are based upon differences in job-related qualifications recognized by the market. Decomposing a market wage into its sex and qualification components is not a simple matter, however.

The eighth circuit properly interpreted a market defense based on qualifications in *Horner v. Mary Institute*.[10] The court found that the wage difference between a male and female physical education teacher existed because the former's "experience and ability made him the best person available for the job and because a higher salary was necessary to hire him. The differential was based on a factor other than sex."[11] The court also stated "it is our view that an employer may consider the market place value of the skills of a particular individual when determining his or her salary."[12]

While that view seems statutorily correct and is certainly a business imperative, its application can be difficult, as shown by *Futran v. RING Radio*.[13] The radio station hired a man and a woman at the same time as talk show hosts, paying the man $9000 more than the woman. The male had a background of greater job experience and public contact than the female plaintiff. However, the court found that "even taken cumulatively the foregoing factors do not form the basis for the wide disparity in salaries."[14] The decision for the plaintiff in this case can hardly be faulted—independent evidence of discrimination against women at the station was found, and the plaintiff turned out to be a more popular announcer than the male. Yet the court's quoted statement raises a troublesome question. How can the court put a value on the market worth of experience and other nonsexual factors? Unless it can do so, at least in close cases, it is not possible to evaluate the defense that an employer's wage differential is based on the market wage for the man's greater experience and other nonsexual factors. In other words, it would be impossible to determine whether the differential is justified by market-valued qualifications or is due at least partially to the fact that the market provides a higher wage for a man than for an equally qualified woman.

A recent trial court decision and its reversal by the ninth circuit have further complicated this separation and the use of a market defense for unequal pay. In *Kouba v. Allstate*[15] the plaintiff alleged that the method used by Allstate for setting its starting salaries for new sales agents resulted in lower salaries for women who were doing the same work as men. Salaries for new sales agents were determined by four criteria: education, ability, experience, and prior salary. Allstate was unable to convince the court that the last element, prior salary, fell within the "any other factor other than sex" exception of the statute, and was also unable to show that all of the existing wage advantages for its male agents were due to the first three, legitimate criteria for wage differentiation. Consequently, the court found for the plaintiff.

The court accepted the plaintiff's argument that a woman's prior salary could well have been depressed by historical discrimination against females. It concluded that Allstate had not met its burden of showing that the plaintiff's prior salary was free from such discrimination and was based on factors other than sex.

> Although the issue is not without its difficulties, it thus appears to me that as a matter of law an employer may not set a salary schedule which differentiates between its male and female employees doing the exact same job, based upon the immediate past salaries paid to the men and women, unless it can demonstrate that it has assessed the previous salaries and determined that they themselves were based on any factors other than sex.[16]

In response to the obvious question that this statement raises—how can an employer determine that a woman's prior salary was based on a factor other than sex—the court wrote, "The effect of this holding is simply to require the employer to ascertain one more piece of information in the course of determining the appropriate 'monthly minimums.' "[17] A subsequent footnote amplified this sentence:

> . . .a prospective employer need not undertake a massive investigation of a previous employer's practices. In the absence of reasons to do otherwise, a subsequent employer may rely upon the information acquired from the previous employer concerning that employer's practices just as he relies upon that employer's information concerning other aspects of the prospective employee's history.[18]

Although the meaning of this statement is not entirely clear, it appears to say that an employer can meet the statutory obligation to determine if a female applicant's prior salary was based on sex or some other factor by simply asking this question of the previous employer. Then the court, although ruling for the plaintiff, provided employers with a trivial procedure for legitimizing their use of prior salary to establish hiring salaries, thus avoiding the reach of the Act. Informed prior employers are not likely to admit that the salary of a former employee was based on sex; rather, they will claim that it was based on schooling, training, experience, or other nonsexual factors.

The ninth circuit reversed the trial court's finding that Allstate had to prove its use of prior salary did not incorporate sex discrimination.[19] The higher court held that prior salary could be used as long as it was justified by "business reasons." The case was remanded for evaluation of the business justifications proffered by the company.

The issue faced by the courts in *Kouba* was whether prior salary can be used to justify unequal salaries to men and women for equal work given the likelihood that it has been influenced by the factor of sex operating through market processes. The lower court recognized that the wage factor "prior salary" could simply be a disguise for unequal wages paid because the market sometimes produces a lower wage for a woman than for a man. (The court cited historical discrimination as a cause of lower market wages for women. The cause can also be nondiscriminatory, i.e., the crowding of women into "light" occupations because of preferences and physiological characteristics.) The lower court ruled, therefore, that Allstate had to show that its use of prior salary did not incorporate the factor of sex into its salary differentials—it had to show that the lower prior salaries of women did not reflect job markets which pay "women less than men for the same work," in the words of the Supreme Court's *Corning Glass* decision.

Evidence to this effect, of course, is extremely difficult to obtain since the salary of any individual is influenced by a large number of qualification and other factors; consequently, the trial court indicated that the employer's burden could be met by merely asking an applicant's previous employer whether her pay was based in any way on her sex. This suggestion for a trivial procedure should not obscure the trial court's recognition that prior salary is likely to incorporate the factor of sex into subsequent salary determination.

The ninth circuit's reversal of the trial court goes against the EPA cases cited earlier in this chapter, including that of the Supreme Court in *Corning Glass*, that prohibited unequal wages based on lower market wages for women than for men.* Although prior salary was not explicitly involved as a wage-setting factor in those decisions, they are material because they prohibited "market" defenses for unequal pay. An attempt to justify unequal wages for women on the ground that their prior salaries were less than those

---

*See also, among other cases, *Hodgson v. Brookhaven General Hospital*, 436 F2d 719 (CA 5 1970); and *Shultz v. First Victoria National Bank*, 420 F2d 648 (CA 5 1969).

of men is also a market defense because of the strong likelihood that a woman's salary history has been influenced by market processes that have produced lower pay for women than for men. In other words, to offer a woman a lower salary than a man because her previous salary was less than his might well be taking advantage of the lesser "bargaining power" of women, to use the phrase of the *Brookhaven* court.[20]

The ninth circuit ruling also conflicts directly with *Neeley v. MARTA*[21], in which a district court held that a policy of limiting the salaries paid to new employees to no more than 10 percent above their prior salaries was prohibited, because society traditionally has paid women less than men. Although the trial courts in both *Kouba* and *Neeley* cited historic discrimination against women as the culprit in the use of prior salary, the more general phenomenon is simply that for a variety of reasons, women are often paid less than similarly qualified men, and unequal wages for equal work cannot be based on this market result under established EPA law.

Evidence of business reasons for use of the prior salary factor does not alter these conclusions. No matter how valid, business reasons cannot obliterate the EPA cases that found market differentials to be an unlawful defense for wage differentials involving equal work, and they cannot obliterate the fact that prior salaries most likely have been established by markets that pay men more than women. The ninth circuit's decision to the contrary is not likely to prevail.

The courts may ultimately prohibit the use of prior salary to establish hiring salaries for new employees, or employers may discontinue the use of this factor if they are required to prove that it is free of sex discrimination. Other criteria can replace it, for example, education, experience, and training, which collectively are highly correlated with prior salary. Still, prior salary does have valuable uses. For example, it can indicate ability that goes beyond characteristics such as education and experience, and it can be a starting point for bargaining over an applicant's hiring salary. Using prior salary for these and other reasons seems likely to become a casualty of the EPA.

MARKET PERVASIVENESS

Relatively few EPA cases have included explicit market defenses for paying men and women unequally, in large part because the courts have clearly prohibited such defenses. Their absence, however, is a misleading fact because in nearly all instances of unequal pay for similar work, whether or not the male and female jobs are found to be substantially equal, the pay differences are due to market forces.

Typically, EPA cases occur where employers believe they have two similar but distinct jobs, one that can be adequately performed by women and one that cannot. Employers may be wrong in these beliefs, and Title VII may require them to hire women for both jobs despite their beliefs. Regardless, they will establish a higher wage for what they think is the male job because they know that it takes a higher wage to employ reliable, long-term male workers than to employ comparable females. Thus the unequal pay comes about because of employer beliefs about the nature of both jobs and the labor market for men and women. (In some cases collective bargaining agreements rather than employer beliefs produce the unequal pay.)

Ironically, the EPA cannot touch those male and female positions that have been sufficiently differentiated so that the equal work standard of the Act does not apply. Therefore, the statute prevent employers from exploiting low market wages for females only where the "female" job cannot be substantially differentiated from the male position, for example, in the cases of salesmen and saleswomen and hospital aides-orderlies. Even in these cases, as some of the court decisions show, it is possible to assign substantially different work tasks to the two sexes; where this has been done, a finding of job equality is unlikely. Thus, it can be argued that the EPA does not significantly alter the employer's exploitation of low market wages for women.

NOTES

1. 436 F2d 719. 726.

2. *Corning Glass Works v. Brennan,* 417 U.S. 188, 205, (1974).

3. Id. 207.

4. Id. 195.

5. 335 F. Supp. 731, 733 (M.D. Fla. 1971), partially affirmed, 488 F2d 443 (CA 5 1973).

6. 479 F2d 235, 241, Note 12 (CA 5 1973).

7. *Wirtz v. Muskogee Jones Store Co.,* 293 F. Supp. 1034, 1039 (E.D. Ok. 1968).

8. 473 F2d 589 (CA 3 1973).

9. Compare Arthur Larson, *Employment Discrimination,* (New York: Matthew Bender, 1982) Vol. I, 7:77–82.

10. 22 EPD 30565 (CA 8 1980).

11. Id. at 14053.

12. Id.

13. 24 EPD 31410 (N.D. Ge. 1980).

14. Id. at 18425.

15. 26 FEP 1273 (E.D. Ca. 1981), filed under Title VII, but decided under the EPA.

16. Id. at 1284.

17. Id.

18. Id.

19. *Kouba v. Allstate Ins. Co.*, 30 FEP 57 (CA 9 1982).

20. 436 F2d 719, 726 (CA 5 1970).

21. 25 EPD 31693 (N.D. Ge. 1979).

7

EQUAL JOB ACCESS AND JOB EQUALITY UNDER THE EPA

Title VII of the Civil Rights Act, enacted one year after the EPA became law, provides a much more comprehensive ban on sex discrimination in employment than does the EPA. The former prohibits discrimination in hiring, promotion, training, and discharge, as well as in compensation. Has Title VII, the nation's most important antidiscrimination statute, influenced the enforcement and interpretation of the EPA, despite, or perhaps because of, the latter's much narrower focus? Before considering the influence of Title VII, another question needs examination. Is there any basis for an EPA claim when women have equal access (equal opportunity) to all jobs in question? This question would exist even if there were no Title VII prohibitions on job discrimination.

STATUTORY INTERPRETATION

The statute itself provides little guidance on this question. Its language is directed strictly to the compensation of the two sexes. Therefore, it could be concluded that an equal pay violation can exist when women have equal access with men to a higher paid job, as well as when they don't. On the other hand, the essence of the Act is to prohibit lower pay to women when they are doing work equal to that of higher paid men. Where equal access exists and both men and women are employed in the higher paid job, it is true that women in the lower paid job are paid less than men, but they are also paid less than women. Consequently, can the wage differential that exists between the two jobs be based on sex? Since women can seek and obtain employment in the better paid job, must not the differential be based on something other than sex?

Given the statute's failure in dealing with this issue, one can turn to its Congressional history for guidance. During the floor debate on the EPA, Congressman Goodell provided support for the view that the EPA does not apply where equal job access is a fact. He stated, "Differences in pay between groups or categories of employees that contain both men and women within the group or category are not covered by this Act."[1]

There are sound public policy reasons for this view, although they cannot be found in the statute itself. Sex discrimination in employment is most evident, and clearly invidious, in the relative absence of women from better paid occupations. When an employer truly integrates men and women on all jobs, it is reasonable to infer that there is no discrimination. In that case the wage differences among the employer's various jobs are unlikely to be based on a desire and ability to exploit female labor. Furthermore, the incentive to open all jobs to both men and women is reduced if the employer who takes this action remains subject to murky claims about the bases of wage differentials among jobs.

The courts have not followed either this reasoning or Congressman Goodell's statement about the intent of the Act. The language of the statute prohibits employers from "paying wages to employees. . .at a rate less than the rate which he pays wages to employees of the opposite sex for equal work. . . ." The courts have interpreted this in a manner that permits women to press an equal pay claim by comparing their work with that of any male employee, whether the male is in a job class that is all male or employs both men and women. Such rulings are so common that there is no need to cite particular cases.

It must be said, however, that in nearly all instances in which the courts have so ruled, there have been comparatively few women employed in the higher paid job class. When women are more fully integrated into the higher paid job, comprising, say one-third or more of the classification, the inference that the employer's wage differentials are nondiscriminatory becomes stronger. This view appears to have prevailed in an unusual case brought under both the EPA and Title VII, where female clerical workers, who had been denied pay raises granted to warehouse workers, alleged wage discrimination based on sex. The district court ruled that the differential wage treatment was not based on sex (the equal work question was not reached), stating, "This is made especially clear by the fact that at the times the allegedly discriminatory raises for the warehouse workers were granted, a substantial number of the warehouse workers were women."[2] Properly stated, the claim in this case was inequitable pay for the lower paid job, but that claim does not properly come under the EPA.

It can be argued that even when both men and women are fully integrated in a higher paid job, the wage differential that exists between it and a lower paid job is still based on sex. The argument would be that the lower paid job is seen by the employer as a "women's job" and is priced accordingly, whereas the higher paid position is viewed as appropriate for either sex and, therefore, carries a higher wage rate. This argument is not consistent with a claim that the two jobs involve equal work, however, unless it is also shown that the employer's perception of the differences between the jobs is wrong. Since the employer's perception of the jobs, brings about a greater wage for one of the jobs than would otherwise be paid, it is not likely to be wrong.

When female employment in the higher paid job is relatively small, there is greater justification for an EPA claim because the employer may not be truly nondiscriminatory. A few women may have been employed in the higher paid job to disguise a wage differential actually based on sex. Again, it is not clear why an employer would pay for equal work at two different wage rates, but it is possible that such a seemingly irrational arrangement exists due to a collective bargaining agreement, employer preferences, or some other reason.

Because of these possibilities, the courts have probably been wise to hear equal pay claims when both men and women are employed in a higher paid job to which a lower paid job is assertedly equal. The plaintiff should bear a heavy burden of proof under such circumstances, however, because the circumstances make it unlikely that the lower paid women are paid less because they are women. Since women are employed in the higher paid job, there should be an initial presumption that it includes work that is different from that of the lower paid job.

JOB ACCESS AND EQUAL WORK DECISIONS

Whether it makes sense or not, the courts do hear EPA claims when women apparently have equal access to both jobs being compared as well as when they do not. An interesting question is whether the existence or absence of equal job access has any influence on the court's judgments about whether the jobs in question are equal and whether there exists an EPA violation. Does equal access of both sexes to two jobs affect the court's judgment as to whether the jobs are equal, and, conversely, does the fact of unequal opportunity for one or both of the jobs affect the equal work judgment?

Nothing in the statute indicates that equal work judgments are to be influenced by the existence or absence of equal job access. However, the previous section makes a logical case for believing that, where equal access truly exists, lower and higher paid jobs do not involve equal work. Furthermore, unequal access ordinarily is a violation of Title VII, and this could influence judgments about equal work through an inference that, if employers discriminate against women in hiring and job assignments, they probably also discriminate against them in compensation. Finally, equal access makes available to women a remedy for their low pay, even if their work is judged unequal to that of a higher paid job; they can ultimately move to the higher paid job. When equal access does not exist, a court judgment of unequal work means that women in a lower paid job must permanently accept their lower pay status or leave their employer. These facts could have an influence on equal work decisions, causing courts to find EPA wage discrimination (through judgments that women are performing equal work) where the upward mobility of women is blocked, and to find no such discrimination where it is not.

Perhaps more important than any of these hypothetical reasons for an equal access-unequal work association is that, under certain circumstances, the existence of equal access provides a direct test of the equality of work of two jobs. When women do have an equal opportunity to apply and be hired for a higher paid job that they assert to be equal to a lower paid one, and they do not exercise this opportunity, a conclusion that the two jobs are not equal would seem to be warranted. In these circumstances, something that is differentially unattractive or difficult, and therefore unequal, about the higher paid job must be keeping women from applying for it. This equal access test is definitive only where equal access truly exists and where women do *not* apply for the higher paid work. If they *do* apply, the jobs could still be unequal in terms of their work requirements because the applications may be induced by the higher wage or some other aspect of the higher paid job. But where many women become employed in the higher paid job, an EPA claim is not likely to be made.

From the court decisions, it is difficult to discern whether job access facts are influencing equal work decisions, because the courts almost never explicitly make a causal connection.* In my judgment, however, job access is important for these decisions, perhaps more important than any other element of evidence. And I believe that the courts are especially influenced by evidence that women have the opportunity to apply, but do not, for the higher paid of two assertedly equal jobs. The courts, appropriately, nearly always view this fact as evidence of the inequality of the two jobs.

EQUAL ACCESS CASES

Aside from the clerical worker cases previously described, I have not found any EPA cases where women in a lower paid job have alleged that

---

*A recent case made it explicit. See *Maguire v. Trans World Airlines,* 535 F. Supp. 1283 (S.D. N.Y. 1982).

their work was equal to that of a higher paid job that employed both men and women in more or less equal proportions.* Possible complainants in such circumstances apparently do not perceive the wage differential as based on sex, or do not believe that a court would so perceive it.

There have been many cases in which equal access and the absence of female applications for a higher paid job have been associated with court findings that two jobs are not equal. The opinions in these cases do not directly connect the fact of equal access and absence of female applications to the finding of inequality. Instead, the judgments of inequality are justified in terms of the statutory standards of skill, effort, responsibility, and working conditions. Nonetheless, these opinions do note the equal access and absence of female applications, and it seems likely that the courts are concluding, but not stating, that the absence of applications by women for the higher paid job is evidence that the two jobs in question are not equal.

A number of cases involving male and female cleaning jobs appear to have tacitly accepted this reasoning. In *Marshall v. National Cleaning Contractors*, the district court first made clear its willingness to entertain an equal work claim where women were employed in the higher paying job: "[T]he fact that small numbers of women occasionally entered the heavy cleaner category and were paid the corresponding salary is not fatal to the Secretary's [of Labor] case.³ The court, however, did decide that the heavy and light cleaning jobs were not equal, and although this conclusion was justified by detailed comparisons of the two jobs, the court did cite statistics showing that very few of the women who had been offered heavy positions had accepted them. Similarly, in *Marshall v. Building Maintenance Corporation* and *Marshall v. Dallas Independent School District*, the courts noted that few women had applied for heavy duty cleaning positions because they considered these jobs to be "more strenuous and unpleasant" or "harder."⁴ Both courts found that the light and heavy cleaning jobs were unequal. This finding was repeated in *Usery v. Columbia University* after the court noted that when Columbia had opened the heavy cleaning job to women in 1972, only seven, of approximately 100 female light cleaners had applied for it. Of these seven, four returned to the light job after seven weeks, and no other women had applied for the heavy job up to the time of trial in 1977, despite the 45-cents-an-hour wage differential that it enjoyed.⁵

Female Preference

Given the apparent lack of female interest in the higher paid job that

---

*While men and women may have been well integrated in the higher paid jobs in *Corning Glass Works v. Brennan*, 417 U.S. 188 (1974), this integration occurred after an EPA charge had been filed.

characterized these cases, one cannot help wondering whether the U.S. Department of Labor, which brought the litigation, had the support of the women who stood, presumably, to benefit. In one instance involving cleaning work, *Marshall v. Kenosha Unified School District*, it is very clear that such support did not exist.[6]

A wage differential between male custodians and female cleaners had existed in the Kenosha school district since 1953, based on job evaulations by the State of Wisconsin's Bureau of Personnel. The evaluations had been repeated in 1965. A collective bargaining agreement between the school district and a union representing its service employees provided for non-discriminatory hiring for the two jobs. Nonetheless, the jobs were largely segregated by sex: in the period 1970–78, four females were employed as custodians and one male had been employed as a cleaner.

Sometime during the six years of proceedings prior to the trial of this case, the school district, in response to an employee inquiry, told its employees that "if the school district is required to pay housekeepers to perform the same duties it expects custodians to perform, and that if a housekeeper is unable to perform the duties which a custodian is expected to perform, that the housekeeper will be terminated by the school district."[7] Subsequently, twenty-nine of thirty-two cleaners then employed petitioned the Equal Employment Opportunity Commission (which had inherited the case when EPA enforcement was transferred from the Department of Labor in 1979) to drop the lawsuit. The EEOC not only refused to do so, it also alleged that the quoted statement from the school district had been coercive. The trial court dismissed this allegation, commenting that the lawsuit "may have been brought ill advisedly," and found the jobs to be unequal. The seventh circuit affirmed this finding and cited as evidence of inequality the petition brought by the twenty-nine cleaners.[8]

It is interesting that the female cleaners attempted to supplement the inferential evidence of job inequality, provided by the near absence of female applications for the custodian job, with more direct evidence by way of a request that the government drop the litigation. The request was obviously motivated by fear of the consequences of a court finding that the two jobs were equal. The women were, no doubt, concerned about their ability to perform the custodial duties or about the effort required to perform them. Yet, even this direct evidence did not convince the government that the jobs were unequal.

Exceptions

There have been very few instances where the courts have found equality between two jobs when equal access of both sexes to both jobs existed and few women applied for the better paid job. One such case was *Shultz v.*

American Can Company—Dixie Products[9] discussed in Chapter 4. The trial court for that case noted that no females had applied for the company's night machine operator job, which required handling heavy rolls of paper in addition to machine work, since it had opened the position to them in 1965. The trial court used this fact to conclude that the company had not discriminated among employees on the basis of sex. Whether that finding influenced the court's additional conclusion that the night and day jobs were not equal is not clear.

On appeal the eighth circuit reversed the trial court and found that the jobs were equal, commenting that the statutory violation that had existed before the night job was opened to women was not "cured" when the open access event took place. The conclusion that opening a higher paid job to women does not remedy an EPA violation was subsequently affirmed by the Supreme Court in its *Corning Glass* decision, but the conclusion in *American Can* did not speak to the prior question of whether equal job access and the absence of female applicants for the higher paid job constituted evidence of the inequality of two jobs. The eighth circuit apparently did not think so. But since the logic behind the question is strong, the court should have explained why the absence of female applicants for American Can's better paid night operator job was not evidence of its inequality with the day operator job.

Usery v. Board of Education of Baltimore County also found equal work where higher and lower paid cleaning jobs were available to both sexes.[10] Only a few women had applied for the higher paid position, and the employer's job evaluation system was the basis for the pay differences; yet the equal work finding was made.

UNEQUAL ACCESS CASES

Nearly all court findings of equal work (and, consequently, of an EPA violation), where the case involved job classes rather than individuals in highly specific employment positions, have been under circumstances where females were blocked from employment in a higher paid job. (The three cases described in Chapter 4—*American Can, Wheaton Glass,* and *Corning Glass*—all fall under that conclusion.* Whether the job discrimination present in these cases influenced the courts' judgments that the female complainants were doing equal work is not made explicit. But the facts are that a finding of equal work is nearly always accompanied by evidence of job discrimination against women, and conversely, evidence of job discrimina-

---

*In *American Can* and *Corning Glass*, equal access to the higher paid job had been established subsequent to the allegation of an EPA violation.

tion against women is almost always accompanied by a finding of equal work. Therefore, it is reasonable to hypothesize that the courts are inferring wage discrimination from evidence of job discrimination.*

A finding of equal work when women are denied access to a higher paid job may not be made where sex appears to be a *bona fide* job qualification (*"bona fide* occupational qualification" in Title VII language), as with aides-orderlies and salespersons, for example. In *Hodgson v. Golden Isles Nursing Home*, the fifth circuit found that aide and orderly jobs were not equal and wrote, "We do not here decide whether the job of orderly should be open to females or whether the job of nurse's aide should be open to males," concluding that the question should be decided under Title VII.[11] *Hodgson v. Robert Hall Clothes Inc.* was similar.[12] Here, sex was a legitimate hiring qualification for the firm's male and female sales positions, meaning women did not have access to the higher paid male positions. Robert Hall argued that a wage discrimination charge under the EPA could not be upheld unless Title VII was also violated. The court rejected that argument, asserting the independence of the two statutes, but it went on to find that the jobs were not equal and that the EPA had not been violated (see Chapter 6).**

These two cases indicate that where women are *lawfully* barred from employment in a higher paying job, the courts will, upon occasion find unequal work and no EPA violation. (Most salesperson decisions have held that the male and female positions were equal.) These cases, then, are exceptions tending to prove the rule that, where there is unlawful discrimination against women in employment for a higher paid job, a finding of equal work and an EPA violation is extremely likely.

THE INFLUENCE OF TITLE VII

After reading EPA cases, the conclusion looms large that, in judging the equality of two jobs, which is most EPA cases are all about, the courts are crucially influenced by evidence about the opportunity of female employees to be employed in the higher paid job. Where women enjoy equal

---

*Job discrimination can also defeat an affirmative defense for a *prima facie* finding of unequal pay for equal work. A number of decisions have held that a training program was not a lawful justification for unequal wages where women were barred from the program. *Shultz v. First Victoria National Bank*, 420 F2d 648 (CA 5 1969) *Hodgson v. Behrens Drug Co.*, 475 F2d 1041 (CA 5 1973); *Hodgson v. Security National Bank of Sioux City*, 460 F2d 57 (CA 8 1972); *Hodgson v. Fairmount Supply Co.*, 454 F2d 490 (CA 4 1972).

**Inequality of male and female sales jobs was also found in *Hodgson v. the Cain-Sloan Co.*, 9 FEP 831 (MD Tenn. 1973), affirmed, 502 F2d 200 (CA 6 1974).

access, findings of job equality are rare. Where the opportunity for women to be employed in the higher paid jobs does not exist, a finding of job equality and an equal pay violation is very likely.

Some numerical evidence for these conclusions can be provided. I examined seventeen cases that involved male and female cleaners (or custodians and janitor-maids) for this purpose. In most instances the court opinion made fairly clear whether women had access to the higher paid of the two cleaning positions; however, in a few instances I had to make this judgment based on more limited information. The following results were obtained:

	Jobs Equal	Jobs Not Equal
Seven cases where equal access existed	1	6
Nine cases where equal access did not exist	8	1
One case where equality of access could not be determined		1

These results and the prior case review suggest that many EPA cases take their cue from Title VII law, more precisely from the Title VII ban on discrimination in the selection of employees. *Wheaton Glass*, among other cases, suggested that the EPA and Title VII needed to be harmonized.[13] It seems that the form of this harmonization has been to find EPA violations where Title VII violations appear to exist, and to not find EPA violations where Title VII appears to have been followed.

Upon occasion, the perceived association between the EPA and Title VII appears to have confused the courts as to which of the two statutes applies to an action filed under the EPA. In *Krumbeck v. John Oster Manufacturing Company* the court was required to decide the equality of male and female inspector positions.[14] In doing so it quoted from *Bowe v. Colgate-Palmolive Company* that each employee must "be afforded a reasonable opportunity to demonstrate his or her ability to perform more strenuous jobs on a regular basis."[15] *Bowe*, however, was a Title VII case where the company had prohibited women from applying for jobs that required the lifting of 35 pounds or more. In quoting this passage, the *Krumbeck* court was making the point that extra duties cannot be a basis for finding two jobs unequal unless women in the lower paid job are given the opportunity to perform the extra duties. But no such requirement is included in the EPA. It is clear that the court derived this requirement from Title VII. In deciding that the two inspection jobs were equal, the *Krumbeck* court wrote that the plaintiff ". . .was capable of performing tests on sheet metal, yet she was never given the opportunity; that work was reserved for males."[16]

In a subsequent EPA case, *Brennan v. Houston Endowment*, the court used nearly the exact words that *Krumbeck* had quoted from *Bowe*, citing the former as the authority for its statement![17] The *Houston* court, in deciding the equality of male and female custodian positions, also stated that "any work assignment bearing a higher wage which includes no women carries the stigma of suspect validity,"[18] and it cited *Wheaton Glass* to the effect that a wage differential based on extra duties can apply only to those "unwilling and unable" to do the work.[19] Finally, the *Houston* court discussed a Title VII remedy that would open the higher paid custodial job to women. It concluded that the issue it had dealt with was equal pay for equal work, which was not a Title VII issue, and consequently, an open access remedy was inappropriate.[20] The latter is a particularly disingenuous conclusion, since the court had obviously been influenced by the Title VII ban on job discrimination in finding that the custodial jobs were equal.

Wheaton Glass (cited in both the *Krumbeck* and *Houston* decisions) has been the source of much confusion about the appropriate relation between the EPA and Title VII. The following passage from *Wheaton*, together with that court's view that the two statutes must be "harmonized," has produced much of the confusion:

> The fact that some female selector packers, unlike some male selector packers, may have been unwilling or unable to do the work of snap-up boys might justify a wage differential between them. But it would still leave open the question why the company did not include under its flexibility requirement the female selector packers who are both able and willing to do the work of snap-up boys.[21]

Again, there is no basis in the EPA for deciding equal work issues on whether or not employees in the lower paid job have been given a chance to do the work of the higher paid job. The court must have been influenced in the quoted passage by the equal job opportunity emphasis found in Title VII. The quoted words have been frequently cited by courts that also appear to be deciding equal work issues, at least partially, on whether equal job access exists.

It is clear that the courts have struggled with the "harmonization" of the EPA and Title VII without resolving the matter.* In *Brookhaven*, the circuit court rejected the U.S. Department of Labor's attempt to bring Title VII law into the EPA case. The court also commented on the *Wheaton* decision as follows:

---

*One aspect has been resolved. In 1981, the U.S. Supreme Court held that Title VII's prohibition on wage discrimination went beyond equal work circumstances as defined in the EPA. *County of Washington v. Gunther*, 451 U.S. 161 (1981).

At least one federal court of appeals has suggested that equal pay should be required for a "male" job and a "female" job which are in fact unequal if the reservation of the higher paid job to males would be impermissable under Title VII. We think that the present case illustrates very well the problems in such an approach.[22]

The *Brookhaven* court opined that the *Wheaton* approach would yield "unfair results," because women frequently do not want employment in the higher paid of two jobs. The court wrote, "The purpose of the EPA and Title VII. . .are not well served by confounding the respective proofs required of plaintiffs."[23]

Despite this view, the courts have indeed confounded the respective proofs of the two statutes. They have, it appears, made the equal job access requirement of Title VII the key element in deciding job equality under the EPA: if women have equal access to two jobs being compared, the jobs are unlikely to be found equal, and if women have been denied equal access, the jobs are likely to be found equal.

NOTES

1. *U.S. Cong. Rec.* 109:9209 (1963).
2. *Salge v. Burdett Co.*, 22 EPD 30877 (S.D. Ind. 1980).
3. 20 FEP 654, 659 (E.D. Pa. 1979).
4. 16 EPD 8153 (DC Conn. 1977); 21 EPD 30334 (CA 5 1979).
5. 568 F2d 953 (CA 2 1977).
6. 22 FEP 1357 (DC WIS, 1979), affirmed 620 F2d 1220 (CA 7 1980).
7. Id. at 1364.
8. 620 F2d 1220, 1226 (CA 7 1980).
9. 424 F2d 356 (CA 8 1970).
10. 462 F. Supp. 535 (D. Md. 1978).
11. 468 F2d 1256 (CA 5 1972).
12. 326 F. Supp. 1264 (D. Del. 1971), modified, 473 F2d 589 (CA 3 1973).
13. *Shultz v. Wheaton Glass Co.* 421 F2d 259, 266 (CA 3 1970).
14. 313 F. Supp. 257 (E.D. WIS 1970).
15. 416 F2d 711, 718 (CA 7 1969).
16. Id., note 14, 264.
17. 7 EPD 9204, 7007.
18. Id. The quoted words are from *Hodgson v. Behrens Drug Co.*, 475 F2d 1041, 1048 (CA 5 1973).

19. Id., note 13, 264.

20. Id., note 17, 7008.

21. Id., note 13, 264.

22. *Hodgson v. Brookhaven General Hospital*, 436 F2d 719, 727 (CA 5 1970). The suggestion attributed to *Wheaton* is, at most, implicit in that opinion.

23. Id., 727.

8

THE EPA AND WAGE DISCRIMINATION UNDER TITLE VII

Because the EPA only prohibits unequal pay in the relatively rare instances of equal work, it has not and cannot have much, if any, impact on the relatively low pay of women, most of which is due to their concentrated employment in low-paying jobs (that also provide low pay to the men employed in them). For this reason, and because the shift of women to higher paid jobs has been slow, the emphasis in sex discrimination issues in recent years has increasingly focused on the low wage rates paid women, but in a much broader context than the EPA, namely under Title VII of the Civil Rights Act.

Women have recently alleged that the low wage rates of predominately female jobs are discriminatory because they result from employer and societal discrimination against women.[1] That discrimination is alleged to take the form of an "undervaluing" of women's work and a corresponding assignment of low wage rates to that work, or, within a market emphasis, the exclusion of women from certain jobs and a consequent increase in labor supply to predominately female occupations, with low wage rates for the latter as the end result.

These allegations, however, have not been easily translated into violations of Title VII's ban on sex-based discrimination. Until 1981, the major barrier in this regard was the courts' ruling that the EPA was incorporated into Title VII (through the Bennett Amendment), so that sex-based wage discrimination claims under the latter had to meet EPA standards, the most important of which is the equal work standard. Thus, Title VII, the nation's broad antidiscrimination statute, provided no greater remedy for women's wage discrimination claims than did the narrowly drawn EPA.

A major breakthrough occurred with the U.S. Supreme Court's 1981 decision in *County of Washington v. Gunther*.[2] Most fundamentally, the

Court ruled that sex-based wage discrimination claims under Title VII did not have to meet the EPA standard of equal work. Women can now pursue charges that their wage rates are discriminatory without having to show that their work is equal to that of higher paid men. This means that the focus of attacks on sex-based wage discrimination will shift from the EPA to Title VII.

In the post-*Gunther* era, the kinds of charges the courts will permit are not clear. Certainly, claims of disparate treatment from which intentional discrimination can be inferred will be entertained. Disparate impact proofs of discrimination may be circumscribed. Perhaps the most important question is whether comparable worth claims—that certain female-dominated jobs are of equal value to certain male-dominated jobs—will be allowed unless they are supplementary to other evidence of intentional discrimination. Regardless of how these issues are finally decided, the law and experience established under the EPA will be influential on the development of broader bans on wage discrmination against women, just as the EPA was influential in retarding the development of wage discrimination law until the *Gunther* decision.

The past and present influences of the EPA on the development of broad-based wage discrimination law have been several. First, the court's unwillingness to permit more than very limited comparable worth comparisons of jobs under the EPA forced women to look to Title VII for a broadening of their allowable wage grievances. Second, as already mentioned, the courts until 1981 held that Title VII sex-based wage claims had to meet EPA standards. Third, now that the allowable wage claims have been broadened, it is likely that the legislative history of the EPA will be used as one of the bases for denying comparable worth claims under Title VII. Fourth, the experience with comparable worth claims under the EPA, while quite limited, has shown that the courts have great difficulty with these claims; therefore, that experience may inhibit court acceptance of such claims under Title VII. Fifth, EPA law, which has rejected market defenses for unequal pay, will make it difficult to use market defenses successfully to rebut broader wage discrimination charges under Title VII.

The implications of these EPA influences will be woven into this chapter's discussion of post-*Gunther* developments in sex-based wage discrimination. The discussion will review the *Gunther* decision itself, then examine probable developments in wage discrimination claims, and conclude with a consideration of market defenses for these new kinds of claims.

COUNTY OF WASHINGTON V. GUNTHER

Before the U.S. Supreme Court's decision of June 1981, in *County of Washington v. Gunther*, claims of sexual discrimination in compensation had to prove equal work between female and male jobs, whether the claim was made under Title VII of the Civil Rights Act or under the EPA. This interpretation existed because Section 703(h) of Title VII (the Bennett Amendment) declares that all sexual wage differences "authorized" by the EPA are also lawful under Title VII, and the courts, uniformly until 1979, held that sexual wage differentials for unequal work were "authorized" by the EPA and therefore could not be found unlawful under Title VII.[3] In short, the courts interpreted Section 703(h) to mean that sex-based wage discrimination claims had to prove equal work.

Relatively few women hold jobs that would permit them to meet the equal work standard. Consequently, prior to *Gunther*, the possibilities for women to remedy wage discrimination through existing antidiscrimination statutes was very limited. This was a frustrating fact for the cause of female economic progress because it meant that wage discrimination litigation was not available to improve significantly the low relative earnings of females. The Supreme Court's *Gunther* decision broadened the possible bases for sex-based wage discrimination claims by ruling that such claims need not always be based upon an assertion of equal work. Thus, *Gunther* opened Title VII as a source of wage discrimination claims for women that goes beyond the narrowly focused EPA.

Apellate Decisions

Three appellate decisions led the way for the high court's finding. In *Gunther v. County of Washington*,[4] the case ultimately decided by the Supreme Court, the ninth circuit held that female jail guards could pursue a wage discrimination claim under Title VII even though they failed to prove that their jobs were equal to those of male guards. The women had alleged sex discrimination under Title VII because their employer's job evaluations had provided a point rating for their jobs that was 95 percent of the rating for the male job, but the women's pay rates had been set at only 70 percent of males'. In *Fitzgerald v. Sirloin Stockade*,[5] the tenth circuit ruled that a female plaintiff could pursue her wage discrimination allegations under Title VII even though her work tasks were not equal to those of the male advertising director whom she had succeeded. Finally, in *IUE v. Westinghouse*,[6] the third circuit held that Westinghouse had violated Title VII because it paid lower wage rates for predominately female job classifications than for equally rated, predominately male ones. The appellate court overruled the trial court's judgment that Westinghouse's actions were lawful because the female and male classifications did not involve equal work.

The Supreme Court's *Gunther* decision has been reviewed extensively elsewhere,[7] consequently, I will comment on it only briefly. The decision should not have surprised those familiar with wage discrimination law because, before it and the three cited appellate decisions, this law was in an indefensible state wherein sex-based wage discrimination allegations could not be pursued, no matter how egregious, unless equal work was also asserted, while the same claims were legitimate if made on the basis of race, national origin, or any of the other prohibited bases of Title VII. Justice Rehnquist, in his *Gunther* dissent, presented a strong case that the Bennett Amendment was, in fact, intended to limit Title VII sex-based compensation discrimination to that set forth in the EPA, and his argument that the Bennett Amendment should be read as prohibiting discrimination claims based on comparable work assertions is unassailable in my opinion.[8] Nonetheless, the majority decision in *Gunther* was proper because, although the major purpose of the Bennett Amendment was to prohibit discrimination claims based on comparisons of dissimilar jobs, there is no evidence to suggest that Congress also wanted to prohibit claims arising from evidence of *intentional* wage discrimination against women. Furthermore, such an intent, addressed only to women, would have been antithetical to the broad remedial purpose of Title VII. Surely, Congress did not intend to prohibit female victims of blatant sex discrimination—for example, a policy of biannual wage increases for males and annual increases for females—from pursuing justice under the purposely broad antidiscrimination provisions of Title VII, particularly since the same policy would be clearly prohibited by Title VII if it were based upon race.

The purpose of Congress in passing Title VII was the comprehensive outlawing of employment discrimination, including compensation on the basis of sex. Its purpose in including the Bennett Amendment was to harmonize Title VII with the previously enacted EPA, but that harmonization was not designed to make lawful intentional wage discrimination against women. Thus, the Supreme Court correctly decided that intentional sex discrimination in compensation is subject to remedy under Title VII whether or not equal work exists.

Comparable Work and Congressional Intent

Although *Gunther* was correct, Justice Rehnquist was also correct when he asserted in dissent that Congress intended through the Bennett Amendment to incorporate more than the four affirmative defenses of the EPA into Title VII.[9] In the first place, these defenses were already available under Title VII.* More importantly, one year before enactment of the Ben-

---

*The majority *Gunther* opinion contended that the fourth affirmative EPA defense, legitimizing wage differentials based on "any other factor other than sex," uniquely adds to Title VII (452 U.S. 161, 170). But this defense is implicit in Title VII; if a wage practice is based

nett Amendment and Title VII Congress had passed the EPA after it had been amended to prohibit unequal pay for "equal" rather than "comparable" work. The sponsors of the legislation stressed the importance of this change in the floor debates (see Chapter 3); it is doubtful that the legislation would have passed without it. Thus, it seems very likely that the principal purpose of the Bennett Amendment was to avoid a broadening of sex-based wage discrimination law to include wage differentials for comparable work. The legislative history of the amendment, as traced by Justice Rehnquist, supports this view.

Justice Rehnquist asserted too much, however, when he wrote that Title VII sex-based wage discrimination claims cannot exist without proof of equal work.[10] The Justice erred by accepting the view ". . .that Congress in adopting the Equal Pay Act specifically addressed the problem of sex-based wage discrimination."[11] It did not. The EPA focuses entirely on wage comparisons for two or more jobs, prohibiting wage differences between them when the jobs are equal, whether or not there is evidence of employer intent to discriminate. Unfair wage differentials are only one kind of wage discrimination, however, and the fact that they were the only kind considered during the Congressional enactment of the EPA should have no bearing on the scope of Title VII, which was intended to ban employment discrimination broadly. In passing the EPA Congress considered and rejected a comparable work standard. It did not, however, consider any form of wage discrimination other than that of wage differentials between jobs, which had been the sole subject of all equal pay legislation introduced since World War II. It is illogical to contend that the Bennett Amendment's harmonization of the EPA and Title VII was intended to remove from the intentionally broad scope of the latter all forms of wage discrimination other than that involving wage differentials. Many other kinds of wage discrimination are possible, involving, for example, methods of establishing wage rates, the size and frequency of wage increases, and the composition of total compensation. Certainly, Title VII was intended to prohibit intentional discrimination in all wage practices, for women as well as other groups; and there is no reason to believe that Congress, in its desire to harmonize the EPA and Title VII, wanted to remove intentional wage discrimination from Title VII where women were concerned.

In summary, Congress considered only wage differences between jobs when it passed the EPA. It decided that the Act would only regulate sexual wage differencs for equal work, and that decision was incorporated into Title VII by the Bennett Amendment. Since Congress had not considered

---

on a factor other than sex, it cannot constitute sex discrimination unless the factor has no connection to business necessity. This principle is the same under the EPA and Title VII. See *Kouba v. Allstate Insurance*, 30 FEP 57 (CA 9 1982).

forms of wage discrimination that could be shown by other than wage differentials when it passed the EPA, the Bennett Amendment could not possibly have constrained the broad-purposed Title VII from dealing with these other forms of wage discrimination.

The *Gunther* decision helped to make sense of sex-based wage discrimination law by opening the door to claims that do not involve equal work. A question remains, however, as to the exact nature of the claims that will be allowed to enter this open door.

WAGE DISCRIMINATION AFTER *GUNTHER*

Disparate Treatment

Gunther and the appellate case, *IUE v. Westinghouse*, illustrate the most straightforward evidence of disparate wage treatment of women and, inferentially, of intentional discrimination against them. In both cases the relationship (ratio) between the wage rates received by employees and numerical evaluations of their jobs was lower for women than for men. In simpler terms, the actual wage rates of the women were less than would have been expected from their job evaluations. Both of these cases were settled before trial, but commentators generally suggest that trials would have produced judgments of intentional discrimination; in both instances, the lower paid female employees' jobs were evaluated as equal or nearly equal to those of males.

The probable defenses in these two cases would have been simply that the employer was able to hire employees for the female jobs at lower wage rates than for the male jobs, regardless of the job evaluations of each. This is a market defense that, as we have seen, is not permitted under the EPA. The extent to which market defenses will be permitted under Title VII wage discrimination claims is an interesting question (that I will discuss below), but it is unlikely that a market defense would have prevailed within the *Gunther* and *IUE* fact situations. It is one thing for employers to say that jobs are priced according to what the market requires, but it is quite something else to say that they are priced according to the market, even though the resulting wage rates conflict with an existing evaluation system. A job evaluation system connotes, either explicitly or implicitly, that the wage rates of jobs will be established by assessing what the jobs are worth, in terms of certain elements such as skill, effort, and responsibility. If these assessments are ignored in order to use low market wage rates for jobs exclusively or predominately filled by women, the inference of intentional discrimination against women seems justified. Employers may contend that, despite job evaluations, their real intent was simply to pay market wages, but they would then have trouble explaining why they went to the trouble of carrying out job evaluations.

While the *Gunther* and *IUE* facts strongly suggest intentional discrimination, the kind of evidence presented in these cases poses difficulties for wage discrimination law. Perhaps the most fundamental problem is that evidence of intent to discriminate would have been missing in both cases if the employers had not established job evaluation systems, but had simply used the labor market to establish wage rates for all of their jobs. No disparate treatment of women would then have existed.

Gunther and *IUE* provide a clear message: if employer conduct job evaluations, they must use them in wage setting or risk a wage discrimination complaint. Undoubtedly, some employers will now decide not to establish a job evaluation system, and that will hurt the cause of wage equity since job evaluation promotes a rate-for-the-job policy that makes it more difficult to set wage rates according to sex or race.

The *Gunther* and *IUE* cases potentially create a great paradox for wage discrimination law. It now appears that Group A employers, who have the same job classifications and pay the same market wage rates as Group B employers, can be charged with wage discrimination because their wage rates for women conflict with women's job evaluations, while Group B employers are nondiscriminatory under the law because they rely entirely on the market and have no job evaluations. The incentives for eliminating job evaluations or manipulating them to coincide with market rates is obvious.

This paradox, however, also raises the question of whether plaintiff-sponsored job evaluations will compel "market rate" employers to carry out their own evaluations in order to defend themselves against comparable worth claims. I present my views on this question in subsequent sections. Here, I will merely state that courts are not likely to permit such claims in the first place, and further, the courts are likely to recognize, as they have done in EPA cases (Chapter 5), that partisan-sponsored job evaluations are too unreliable to be admitted as evidence for wage discrimination claims.

Christiansen v. Iowa. What does and does not constitute intentional discrimination will not be easy for courts to decide in post-*Gunther* cases. In *Christiansen v. Iowa*,[12] a pre-*Gunther* decision, the University of Northern Iowa established a job evaluation system to provide equitable pay rates for office (female) and physical plant (largely male) jobs. Many of the physical plant jobs, however, could not be filled at the wage rates established by this system. Consequently, the University raised the hiring rates for the physical plant positions above the levels called for by the job evaluations. The eighth circuit said that this was not discrimination because the deviation from the job evaluation rates was based on market necessity, not sex. Whether the facts of *Christiansen* differ significantly from those of *Gunther* and *IUE* is a matter of judgment. All three cases involved failure to pay wage rates that were consistent with employer-conducted job evaluations, with a consequent increase in male-female wage differentials. In *Christiansen*, women were not paid less than their job evaluations called for, but men were paid more than their evaluation rates, whereas in *Gunther* and *IUE* women received less than the wage rates dictated by their evaluations. The eighth circuit concluded, perhaps rightly, that the University was forced by the market to pay above the evaluated rates for certain male positions and that sex was not a consideration in this action. But could not the employers in *Gunther* and *IUE* argue, analogously, that cost constraints required them to pay women their market wage rates, which were less than the wage rates that corresponded to their job evaluations? The County of Washington, as a public jurisdiction, was presumably under a budget constraint, and Westinghouse must compete partially on a price (and thus, cost) basis in the electrical industry.

Business need was the basic motivation in all three of these cases. In *Gunther* and *IUE*, minimizing costs was the need that was met. In *Christiansen*, it was the need to hire quality workers. *Gunther* and *IUE* may be distinguished from *Christiansen* because in the former women received less than they were implicitly promised under employer job evaluation systems, while in *Christiansen* the men received more than promised, but the distinction is a rather subtle one.

Taylor v. Charley Brothers. After *Gunther*, will courts rely on evidence of job segregation to infer intentional sex-based wage discrimination? In *Taylor v. Charley Brothers*,[13] the court inferred wage discrimination against the female employees of segregated female departments on the bases that (1) women were excluded from the high-paying male departments, and (2) the employer had not conducted job evaluations to assess the relative worth of the male and female jobs. Charley Brothers clearly discriminated against women in job assignment, but that fact, by itself, carries no implications for wage discrimination unless one accepts the overly broad generalization that if employers discriminate in job assignment, they must also discriminate in the payment of wages. Generally, women who are confined to certain of an employer's jobs are paid prevailing market wages for those jobs. This is job discrimination, not wage discrimination, and can be remedied by job transfers and back pay for the wages lost due to job segregation. With respect to job evaluations, nothing compels employers to conduct them and many do not. Since there are many reasons for not having job evaluations, their absence cannot be attributed to an intent to discriminate. The trial court in *Charley Brothers* received evidence of job discrimination and nothing more.

In the post-*Gunther* era, distinctions between disparate treatment that proves intentional discrimination and an employer policy of paying what has to be paid to hire workers—a market policy—will be difficult for courts to make, and uneven judgments are likely to result. More unevenness will arise because employers who use a simple market rate policy will be comparatively free from claims of intentional discrimination, compared to those who have a job evaluation system but depart from it to pay market rates when they are below the evaluation rates.

Disparate Impact

Opinions differ as to whether the courts will permit disparate impact proofs of sex-based wage discrimination after *Gunther*.[14] The division exists because Justice Brennan, in his *Gunther* majority opinion, suggested that the incorporation of the Equal Pay Act's fourth affirmative defense (justifying equal pay that is based on "any other factor other than sex") into Title VII may require that the structure of sex-based wage discrimination claims under the latter be different from that of other Title VII litigation.[15] More precisely, *Griggs* type disparate impact proofs of wage discrimination may not be allowed.[16]

It is unlikely, however, that the disparate impact doctrine will be completely excluded from Title VII wage litigation. Under the EPA the nonsexual factors that can legitimize unequal pay do not include literally "any" factor, but only those reasonably connected to business necessity.[17] Thus, under the EPA, a disparate impact case, in effect if not in form, can be made from, for example, a policy of paying military veterans more than other workers. An employer would be hard put to show that this factor is business related. Surely, under Title VII the courts will find discrimination in sexual wage differences that result from facially neutral practices that have nothing to do with business efficiency.

Two district court cases support this view. In *Neely v. MARTA*,[18] a district court ruled that the defendant's policy of requiring executive approval for starting salaries of more than 10 percent above the employee's prior salary was a *prima facie* violation of Title VII because it had a disproportionate impact on the salaries of women, due to their historically low market wages. In *Bryant v. International School Services*,[19] the third circuit accepted the plaintiff's contention that a policy of offering teachers hired in Iran inferior benefits to those hired in the U.S. could have a discriminatory impact on married women. Actual evidence of such an impact was not found, however.

The simplest kind of disparate impact claim would be that the comparatively low salaries paid for predominately female jobs within a given establishment prove the discriminatory impact of whatever practices the establishment uses to fix wage rates.[20] Such claims will not be allowed, however, because if anything, they speak to job segregation rather than wage discrimination, as discussed previously. More specifically, an argument that the policy of setting wage rates according to prevailing market rates has a disparate impact because of the market disadvantages of women will not be accepted because it goes beyond the intent of Title VII and proposes a major change in the existing system of wage determination.

More realistic is a disparate impact (or treatment) claim based on a regression analysis of wage rates for job classifications. In one proposal, if the schooling and experience requirements of job classes fail to explain the wage differences between male- and female-dominated jobs, courts should consider this proof of disparate impact.[21] There are many weaknesses in this proposal, the major one being that many nondiscriminatory factors other than schooling and experience go into setting a wage for a job.

The most sophisticated approach to a disparate impact claim would be a full-scale regression analysis attempting to show that, after all possible wage determination factors are controlled, women are paid less than men.[22] This is not the place to analyze fully this kind of approach. Briefly, I believe that it usually provides evidence of job discrimination—in job assignment and promotion—rather than wage discrimination. Women may not have access to the better-paid jobs within a firm, and this is discriminatory. But usually the wage rates for the jobs occupied by women are not set discriminatorily; rather they are set impersonally, to meet prevailing market rates, or through a system of job evaluation.

It can, of course, be argued than using the market to set wage rates for various jobs contributes to the low pay of women, because market rates for the jobs women prefer and can qualify for are low, partly due to historical job and social discrimination against women. But buying labor, as well as everything else, at market rates is the way most employers do business in the United States, and the courts, by themselves, are unlikely to overturn that practice.

Comparable Worth

"Pure" comparable worth (or work) claims assert that a female-dominated job is worth as much to an employer as a male-dominated comparison job, or is worth some proportion of the male job. Consequently, the argument goes, equal or proportionate wages should be paid for the two jobs. The assertion is usually based on a comparison of the requirements for the positions in question, often in terms of the skill, effort, responsibility, and working conditions criteria of the EPA. The court is asked to order the payment of the equal or proportionate wage.

Thus, *Gunther, IUE,* and *Christiansen* were not comparable worth cases, because the plaintiffs sought merely to enforce the job evaluation results produced by the defendant employers' own systems, claiming that the failure of the employers to follow these results was intentional discrimination. The plaintiffs did not ask the courts to find their jobs equal in value (worth) to male jobs but, rather, asked that the employers be required to compensate the jobs equally, based upon the equal value determinations that had already been made by means of employer-sponsored job evaluations.*

Lemons v. City and County of Denver,[23] on the other hand, was a pre-*Gunther* comparable-worth case because the plaintiff nurses asked the court to order the City and County of Denver to set nurses' salaries, not on the basis of the salaries paid to other nurses in the community, but based on the local labor market salaries paid in occupations other than nursing. The plaintiffs in *Lemons* made two assertions: (1) that nurses' salaries are depressed because of sex discrimination, and (2) that nurses' jobs are of equal worth to many higher paid jobs in the community. The court did not reject these assertions but did deny relief to the plaintiffs, because Title VII does not require ". . .an employer to ignore the market in setting wage rates for genuinely different work classifications."[24]

Gerlach v. Michigan Bell Telephone Company[25] was a pre-*Gunther* rejection of a comparable worth claim at the district court level. Female Engineering Layout Clerks contended that their jobs were of equal worth to the higher paid male job of Field Assistant, but the court concluded that Title VII does not authorize the courts "to undertake an evaluation and determination of the relative worth of employees."[26] This conclusion was based partly on the court's view that Congress clearly did not intend to permit comparable worth claims under the Equal Pay Act.

Taylor v. Charley Brothers,[27] also decided prior to *Gunther*, was not a comparable-worth case, but it does illustrate how a comparable-worth claim can be successfully combined with evidence of intentional sex-based discrimination. The district court found that Charley Brothers had practiced various kinds of job discrimination against women—assignment, segregation, promotion, etc.—and, therefore, inferred that they were also discriminating in the wages paid women. It went on the conclude, based on the plaintiff's job evaluation, that certain female warehouse workers have previously criticized this court's inference of intentional wage discrimination an unwarranted. Regardless, its judgment about the relative worth of different jobs seems unwise. Job evaluations, even when they rely upon presumably objective observations of work tasks, consist ultimately of subjective judgments about the comparative worth of these tasks.[28] Most EPA decisions have recognized that fact by giving little weight to job evaluations in deciding equal work questions, whether they were conducted by plaintiffs or defendants (Chapter 5). The court for *Charley Brothers,*

---

*This factual description also fits the recently decided *AFSCME v. State of Washington*, No. C82-465T (E.D. Wash. 1983).

having already inferred wage discrimination against the plaintiffs, apparently accepted their job evaluations as confirmation of its judgment. Then, vast differences existed in the kinds of evidence available for the two findings of job and wage discrimination. Factual evidence regarding the hiring, assignment, transfer, promotion, and segregation of women supported the finding of job discrimination, while only inference from these facts and job evaluations—subjective evidence—supported the finding of wage discrimination.

If *Charley Brothers* is followed, competing, partisan job evaluations could be expected in subsequent wage litigation. Then, how would the courts choose between them? *Charley Brothers* itself gives an answer, but an unsatisfactory one, in my opinion. The court considered a post-litigation company job evaluation, as well as the evaluation evidence submitted by plaintiffs during the trial, for the purpose of judging the appropriate wage rates of the female employees. The court ultimately preferred the plaintiff's evaluation plan for the following reasons:

> . . .plaintiffs' expert employed a job evaluation plan which has been more widely used and tested over a longer period of time than defendants' expert's job evaluation plan. Also, the job evaluation plan utilized by the plaintiffs' expert contained more discrete categories of analysis, which were more carefully defined, than the plan utilized by defendants' expert which was largely subjective. Finally plaintiffs' expert had far more experience in the field of job evaluation than defendants' expert.[29]

These reasons are not convincing. They fail to take into account that evaluation results are ultimately a matter of subjective judgment no matter how widely or long the plan has been used, the number of discrete categories (factors) included, or the experience of the expert who makes the judgments. Courts need to recognize that, given the subjective nature of the evaluation process, the litigating party that hires the expert is likely to be a more important influence on the evaluation outcomes than any of the elements cited in the quoted passage. Fortunately, *Charley Brothers* is not likely to serve as precedent for the use of job evaluations in comparable-worth cases, in part because of its unwarranted inference of wage discrimination from job discrimination.[30]

Briggs v. City of Madison,[31] decided after *Gunther*, has provided the greatest court acceptance yet of a comparable-worth claim. In this case, the public health nurses (female) of Madison sued the City, alleging that their jobs required qualifications at least equal to those required for the City's sanitarian (male) position, and that the higher pay for the latter was evidence of intentional sex discrimination. The court received evidence of the equal worth of the two jobs, found that they did, in fact, have equal requirements, and concluded that the plaintiffs had made out a *prima facie* case of intentional sex-based wage discrimination. The court went on to credit the employer's defense that the wage differential between the nurses and sanitarians was due to market exigencies, but that does not lessen the significance of its acceptance of a *prima facie* case entirely on the basis of a claim of comparable worth.

The court attempted to limit this significance by distinguishing the nurses' claim from prior cases, which had rejected comparable-worth assertions. The opinion contended that there was "a substantial similarity of work requirements and work conditions"[32] for nurses and sanitarians, in contrast to *Lemons*, where nurses had sought comparisons with diverse occupations. This point fails, however, because the job descriptions for nurses and sanitarians, included in the court opinion, make it evident that the duties are different: nurses provide assistance with personal health needs in a variety of circumstances and conduct health education, while sanitarians largely inspect establishments for compliance with health regulations. There was no contention that the two jobs could be considered equal under the EPA, thus the court's finding that they had equal requirements and value was clearly the *prima facie* acceptance of a comparable-worth claim.

Power v. Barry County,[33] also a post-*Gunther* case, is in direct contrast to *Briggs*. Here, matrons for county female prisoners claimed comparable worth with male correction officers who supervised jail inmates. The matrons also performed dispatcher duties. The district court cited *Lemons* and *Gerlach* as authority, distinguished *Gunther* and *IUE*, and decided that comparable worth is not "a cognizable and independent cause of action." The decision stated:

> A review of the legislative history of Title VII leads me to conclude that the Supreme Court's recognition of intentional discrimination may well signal the outer limit of the legal theories cognizable under Title VII. There is no indication in Title VII's legislative history that the boundaries of the Act can be expanded to encompass the theory of comparable worth. Nor is there convincing evidence that Congress inteded to make such a theory available to those seeking redress for real or imaginary wage inequalities. Nothing in the legislative history indicates support for an independent claim of recovery where the outcome of the case is dependent upon a court's evaluation of the relative worth of two distinct jobs.[34]

These views, rather than the acceptance of an independent comparable-worth claim, as in *Briggs*, are likely to prevail among the courts in their post-*Gunther* treatment of comparable worth.

THE MARKET AS A DEFENSE FOR WAGE DIFFERENTIALS

Wage discrimination litigation has become more likely following the

Gunther decision, although the forms that the litigation will take are not yet determined. One thing about the increased litigation is likely: it will test the market as a defense for wage differentials between male and female jobs and, in the process, will produce much debate about economic ideology and the nation's commitment to a market-oriented economic system.

A market defense against wage discrimination charges will be common because the wage differentials among jobs in any firm arise largely as a concomitant of the firm's hiring different kinds of workers in the labor market. Most firms operate in more or less competitive labor markets, where prevailing rates are determined by various supply and demand forces, and where any one firm has little ability to influence market rates. This is not to say that labor markets are classically competitive. Indeed, institutional influences are pervasive, but they tend to operate through the supply of and demand for labor. Thus, the single firm takes wage differences as "given" by the market.

Even when a firm uses a job evaluation system to set wage rates and concomitant wage differentials, market influences remain strong. In the first place, job evaluation systems tend to operate with one eye on the market. That is, evaluators know approximately the going rates for the jobs they evaluate, and that knowledge influences their evaluations so that they are likely to be consistent with the market.[35] Second, job evaluation points must be "priced" in the market. Only benchmark or key jobs are priced, but that is enough to ensure that the evaluated wage rates for a firm's jobs are generally consistent with the marketplace. Third, it is a common practice for firms to raise, by one rationale or another, the wage rates of jobs whose evaluated rates are below market rates. The reason for this seemingly hypocritical practice is, of course, to enable the firm to hire and retain workers, to meet market requirements, in other words.

Wage differentials in firms are also established through collective bargaining. Again, however, it is likely that the resulting wag differences between jobs are at least broadly consistent with market rates, especially with respect to the wage differences between predominately male and predominately female jobs.

There are, of course, reasons why the apparently independent wage determination systems of job evaluation and collective bargaining produce wage structures that largely mirror the labor market. First, unless employers pay the market wage, they will have trouble hiring and retaining satisfactory employees. Second, while employers can pay above market wages, few choose to do so because the resulting higher labor costs either reduce their profits or raise their prices. Noncompetitive conditions do occasionally permit above-market rates, but by definition—market rates are those paid by most employers—these are exceptions to the general rule that firms must pay prevailing market wages. The view that wage structures produced by job evaluation and collective bargaining are independent of labor markets is a myth, and the general defense of American employers for their male-female wage differentials must be the labor market.

Intentional Discrimination

Whether the market defense will be accepted by the courts, and under what circumstances, are interesting and important questions. I have already pointed out that, where there is strong evidence of intentional discrimination, as in *Gunther* and *IUE*, a market defense is unlikely to succeed. When males are paid what the employer's job evaluations say they are worth and females are paid less than the job evaluations say they are worth, courts are unlikely to let the market legitimize this inconsistency.

I have also noted that, in *Christiansen*, a market justification for paying men more than their evaluated rates and a consequent increase in the wage differential between male and female jobs was permitted. The rule that seemingly can be drawn from these three cases is that a sexual wage differential established by paying men above their evaluated rates in order to meet market wages is lawful, while a differential produced by paying women less than their evaluated rates but equal to their market rates is not. One reason why this rule is unlikely to prevail, however, is that it can be easily evaded. For example, where a female's and a male's job are evaluated equally, an employer could use the market rate for women as the basic wage for both positions and then pay men above this basic wage to meet their higher market wage. It seems likely, therefore, that the courts will overrule *Christiansen* and find discrimination whenever male and female jobs are evaluated equally but paid unequally.

Comparable Worth

I have stated earlier my view that the courts are likely to follow *Power v. Barry County* and refuse to authorize comparable-worth claims as an independent charge under Title VII.   Nonetheless, there are several reasons for discussing market defenses to comparable worth and related claims. First, my judgment that the courts will reject pure comparable-worth claims may turn out to be wrong, as in *Briggs*. Second, the courts may permit disparate impact proofs of sex-based wage discrimination. If so, the principal defense employers will use to justify their wage differentials between predominately male and predominately female jobs will undoubtedly be the labor market. Third, as in *Charley Brothers*, a comparable worth claim may be combined with independent evidence of intentional discrimination. Market defenses for the wage differentials wil then be employed, at least to rebut the comparable-worth proportion of a *prima facie* case.

Market defenses for wage differentials between different jobs will ultimately test the nation's commitment to a market-oriented economic system. Employers pay secretaries less than salesmen because they can hire them for less, whether or not they also rationalize the pay difference with job evaluations. If the courts permit plaintiffs to present their own job evaluations, as in *Briggs*, and they show, for example, that the requirements for and worth of secretary positions are as great as those of sales positions, the courts will be forced to consider whether the traditional pay basis for hiring employess—whatever it takes to get them—will have to yield to female demands for equity. The female demands, of course, will be accompanied by the argument that the market rates for secretaries and other female occupations are depressed by societal discrimination against women.

The pre- and post-*Gunther* comparable-worth cases thus far decided apparently indicate that the market will be a formidable defense to pure and partial comparable-worth claims. Although *Christiansen* was not a pure comparable-worth case, because the employer had already conceded that the male and female jobs were of equal or nearly equal value, it accepted market requirements as justification for higher wages for the male jobs. In *Lemons*, the tenth circuit seemed to agree that nurses perform work requiring as much skill, effort, and responsibility as many higher paid jobs, but it also concluded that Title VII permits employers to use the market to set wage rates for their various jobs. In *Briggs*, the district court, after finding that the Madison nurses had presented a *prima facie* case of wage discrimination based on evidence of the equal requirements of nurses and santiarians, found for the employer because of his showing that the pay advantage of the sanitarians was "the result of perceived difficulties in the recruitment and retention of persons qualified to perform this particular job."[36]

The court's responses in *Briggs* to two plaintiff arguments against the market as a defense for the nurse-sanitarian wage differential are worth nothing because these arguments are certain to be made again in subsequent cases. The plaintiffs argued first that "the market reflects the biases and stereotypes of the value of women's work and in particular, reflects the devaluation of nurses' salaries resulting from female domination of the nursing field."[37] The court agreed that discrimination has contributed to the low salaries of women but noted that other influences, such as "crowding" and the absence of collective bargaining, have also contributed. More important, however, was the court's conclusion about employer liability under Title VII. The opinion stated:

Under Title VII, an employer's liability extend only to its own acts of discrimination. Nothing in the Act indicates that the employer's liability extends to conditions of the marketplace which it did not create. Nothing indicates that it is improper for an employer to pay the wage rates necessary to compete in the marketplace for qualified job applicants. That there may be an abundance of applicants qualified for some jobs and a dearth of skilled applicants for other jobs is not a condition for which a particular employer bears responsibility.[38]

The nurses' second argument against the market pointed to the EPA cases that have held that unequal pay for equal work cannot be defended on the ground that women can be hired for less than men. The court found these cases "inapposite" because they involved "essentially identical skills," rather than the "closely related" skill and "substantially similar" levels of schooling and training involved in the nurse-sanitarian work comparisons. "Where. . .different skills are required for the performance of the jobs, the employer may explain and justify an apparent illegal wage disparity by showing that persons possessing the requisite skills are commanding higher wage rates in the local market."[39]

The *Briggs* court said, in effect, that the market cannot justify unequal pay for equal work, but it can justify unequal pay for different work, even when the different work has been shown to be equal with respect to the required level of skills, etc. Why Congress would outlaw a market defense in the first case and permit it in the second was not explained, however. It could be argued that Congress considered unequal pay for equal work a more egregious act against women than unequal pay for work on an equal (comparable) level of skills, effort, etc. But it is doubtful this argument can overcome certain critical conclusions about the market that are found in EPA cases.

In *Corning Glass*, the Supreme Court wrote that the EPA was enacted to remedy "a serious and endemic problem in private industry—the fact that the wage structure of many segments of American industry has been based on an ancient but outmoded belief that a man, because of his role in society, should be paid more than a woman even though his duties are the same."[40] The Court also quoted the second circuit's statement that Congress enacted the EPA "recognizing the weaker bargaining power of many women and believing that discrimination in wage rates represented unfair employer exploitation of this source of cheap labor."[41] After these conclusions about the status of women in the labor market, the Court found that Corning's wage differential between its male and female inspectors may have been economic, but was certainly unlawful.[42]

Now that the Supreme Court has ruled that the labor market, because of its discriminatory treatment of women, cannot serve as a defense to unequal pay for equal work, can be the market be used to justify unequal wages between male and female jobs shown to be equal in terms of job qualifications? I do not think so. If the disadvantaged treatment of women in the labor market prevents a market justification of unequal pay for equal work, then the same logic should prohibit a market defense for unequal pay between two jobs that a court finds to be equal in terms of the level of qualifications required. EPA decisions have, in my judgment, greatly restricted the use of a market defense for wage differentials that are *prima facie* discriminatory under Title VII.

Briggs was unpersuasive in attempting to distinguish the market defenses in the EPA cases from a market defense for a comparable-worth claim. *Briggs* was correct in stating that Title VII does not prohibit employers from using the labor market to set wage rates, despite the historical discrimination that has depressed the market wages of women. But neither does the EPA prohibit employers from using the market, yet the courts have refused to allow market defenses in EPA cases because the market wages of women incorporate the historical discrimination that Congress intended to remedy (partially) by the EPA. The logic for similar treatment of market defenses in Title VII case is compelling, *Christiansen* notwithstanding.*

If, as I believe, market defenses for comparable worth and related claims have been vitiated by EPA decisions, judicial treatment of the initial claims themselves becomes extremely important. If the courts permit comparable-worth evidence to establish a *prima facie* case of wage discrimination, as in *Briggs*, a market defense will be of no avail for the *Christiansen*). Thus, the legal future of comparable worth depends upon whether the courts find that Congress intended to permit such claims under Title VII.

I have started earlier my view that *Power* is right and *Briggs* wrong on that question. The legislative history of the EPA and the Bennett Amendment show that, so far as simple wage comparisons are concerned, Congress intended in both the EPA and Title VII, to permit only sex-based discrimination claims when equal work is involved (but also intended to prohibit under Title VII intentional acts of discrimination that can affect wage differentials). This was first shown when Congress explicitly rejected a comparable-work standard in the EPA, and it was shown again one year later when the Bennett Amendment was added to Title VII to harmonize that legislation with the EPA.

In rejecting comparable-worth claims, Congress in effect endorsed the continued use of the market by employers who must establish wage rates for various jobs, because wage differences among a firm's jobs are largely the product of market forces. This conclusion can be reconciled with the courts' conclusion that the EPA was passed to abrogate the workings of the

---

*I read *Lemons* (cited at note 21) not as precedent for a market defense, but, rather, for refusal to entertain a comparable worth claim, even though the refusal was based on deference to the market system of wage determination.

9

FINAL OBSERVATIONS AND CONCLUSIONS

Enforcement of the EPA during the first fifteen years of its existence was the responsibility of the Wage and Hour Division of the U.S. Department of Labor. That responsibility was transferred to the Equal Employment Opportunity Commission (EEOC) in 1979 as part of the consolidation of antidiscrimination statutory enforcement under the EEOC.

Information on the results of enforcement efforts is difficult to obtain, especially from the EEOC. A little is provided in Table 9-1. As a result of the administrative actions of the enforcement agencies, approximately 300 thousand employees were found to be underpaid under the Act from 1965 to 1982, with close to (the data are incomplete) $200 million due them in back pay. The number of employees actually compensated and the monies collected, after litigation and out of court settlements with employers, was considerably smaller, however. From 1973 to 1982, about $55 million was actually received by approximately 110 thousand workers. During the last seven years of the Department of Labor enforcement of the Act, 1973-79, 15 thousand employees a year received back pay, and the average amount of earnings collected annually was $6 million. Thus, the average remedial payment per employee was about $400. The EEOC reported a small number of employee beneficiaries (1,661) of EPA enforcement in 1981, but a comparatively large average back pay benefit of $1,260.

The most substantial enforcement results appear to have been in the mid-1970s, when approximately 17 thousand employee beneficiaries were found each year. By the last year of Department of Labor enforcement (1979), this number had fallen to 11,600. A precipitous drop in enforcement results occurred after the EEOC assumed responsibility for the EPA, with only $5 million restored to employees during 1980-82. This compares with restored wages of roughly $6-9 million in each of the last six years of Department of Labor administration.

118

Table 9-1
Equal Pay Enforcement: Department of Labor 1965-79,
EEOC 1980-82*

Fiscal Year	Employees Found Underpaid	Earnings Due (000)	Earnings Employees	Restored Amount (000)
1965	960	$ 156		
1966	6633	2,098		
1967	5931	3,252		
1968	6622	2,448		
1969	16100	4,585		
1970	17719	6,119		
1971	29992	14,843		
1972	29022	14,030		
1973	29619	18,006	17331	$ 4,626
1974	32792	20,624	16768	6,841
1975	31843	26,485	17889	7,474
1976	27012	19,440	18493	8,532
1977	19382	15,512	12977	6,773
1978	18376	15,971	14929	8,715
1979	14070	10,252	11595	6,423
1980				1,200
1981			1661	2,100
1982				1,700

*Not included are $13,300,000 paid to 13,100 employees in 1973 and 1974 by AT&T for equal pay violations. This back pay was obtained as part of a broad consent decree with AT&T. (Note: Spaces indicate no figures available.)

Source: U.S. Department of Labor and Equal Employment Opportunity Commission.

These figures demonstrate that some women (and a small number of men) have received higher pay and remedial wages as a result of the EPA. Undoubtedly, other women have benefitted from voluntary employer compliance with the Act. But even if the number who have benefited by voluntary action is many times larger than those helped through administrative and legal action, it is evident that only a tiny fraction of the nation's 45 million employed women have been affected by the EPA.

Further, as shown by Table 9-1 and by the fact that compliants under the EPA are now running at about 1,400 a year compared to well over 2,000 a year in the mid-1970s, the results of enforcement efforts under the EPA are declining rapidly. Two explanations exist for this decline. The first is that substantial compliance with the EPA and, to a lesser extent, Title VII has now been achieved, through (1) payment of equal pay for equal work, (2) differentiation of the work tasks of "female" and "male" jobs, and (3) movement of women into traditional male jobs, at least on a token basis.

The second explanation for the decline in enforcement results is that the EEOC is less effective in enforcing the Act than was the Department of Labor. The latter had a major advantage. It was able to couple EPA enforcement with its enforcement of wage and hour requirements under the Fair Labor Standards Act. Consequently, many EPA violations were uncovered during the course of routine wage and hour investigations, including investigations initiated by the Wage and Hour Division itself. The EEOC, on the other hand, is a complaint-oriented agency that infrequently initiates discrimination charges itself.

It is likely that both greater employer compliance and the administrative shift from the Department of Labor to the EEOC have contributed to the decline in enforcement results. The latter is the more important reason, judging from Table 9-1, but a decline in enforcement results was under way even before the administrative shift took place.

The Equal Pay Act receives only minor attention within the EEOC's total enforcement effort. In 1981, there were 1,757 EPA charges received by the Commission, compared to over 11,000 under the Age Discrimination in Employment Act, and nearly 80,000 under Title VII of the Civil Rights Act.[1] In the same year, 50 EPA court cases were filed, compared to 89 under the Age Act and 229 under Title VII.[2]

CONCLUSIONS

Conclusions about the application and interpretation of the EPA have been presented throughout this volume. The most important of these are summarized here:

1. There existed relatively little unequal pay for equal work when the EPA was passed in 1963. Some did exist under collective bargaining agreements and in occupations such as sales, where sex was thought to be a *bona fide* requirement for certain positions, so that men and women were not substitutes for each other. By the 1980s, litigation activity suggested that unequal pay for equal work was rarely found among job classifications but did continue to exist for individual women employed in highly specific positions for which wages and salaries were flexible.

2. The EPA has had very little, if any, impact on female earnings in the aggregate. There is no conclusive evidence on this point, but enforcement results have been miniscule and the male-female earnings gap has not been narrowed.

3. The Act is difficult to apply and enforce because the courts (and anyone else) have trouble deciding what constitutes equal work under the statute. Consequently, EPA decisions are frequently arbitrary and inconsistent.

4. Many EPA decisions appear to confound job discrimination and wage discrimination and to rely upon Title VII prohibitions against the former.

5. As it has been applied by the courts, the EPA, has limited employers' use of labor market wage rates, producing higher labor costs and, conceivably, some shift from male to female employment. (No evidence of the latter effect has been uncovered.) The total effect, must have been slight, however, since the applicability of the Act has been so limited.

6. Both the legislative history of the EPA and the difficulties the courts have experienced in equal work determinations will restrain court acceptance of comparable-worth wage discrimination claims under Title VII. If comparable-worth claims were to be accepted, however, market defenses for the wage differentials under attack would become, at least gradually, unavailing due to the EPA decisions that have rejected market defenses for unequal pay.

Most succinctly, I conclude that the courts have had great difficulty applying the EPA to actual job facts and circumstances, but this difficulty has been of little consequence owing to the limited scope of the law. It is also true that the Act has provided back pay and higher wages to a certain number of women. I do not underestimate the importance of those benefits to the women who received them; I merely conclude that they have been insufficient to produce a noticeable effect on women's earnings generally.

The most immediate lesson to be learned from the EPA experience is that it is difficult to deal legislatively and judicially with wage discrimination, as contrasted with job discrimination. The latter involves an employer decision to discharge or refuse to hire or promote someone on the basis of sex, race, etc. Presumably, the employer has made a conscious decision, and relevant facts will indicate whether the decision was a discriminatory one. In some situations, wage setting may be similar; a wage is offered to a female job applicant and facts may show that the offered wage was less than that paid to a male predecessor. But most often wage discrimination is more difficult to identify. A wage is offered to a female and no facts about alternative wages offered or paid males are available. How can one conclude that the wage offered the woman is discriminatory? Alternatively, an employer establishes for a job classification a wage rate designed to draw in an adequate quantity and quality of applicants, and principally women apply for the job. Even if the wage is relatively low, how is it discriminatory? The employer simply offered a certain wage and hired from the applicants that the market produced.

In neither of these illustrative cases is it likely that a nondiscriminatory wage could be identified to compare with the allegedly discriminatory one. A virtue of the EPA is that it simplifies that matter, even though the determination of equal work remains difficult. The nondiscriminatory wage is that paid to men in the same establishment who are performing work equal to that of certain females. But where equal work does not exist, the nondiscriminatory wage for women who are performing certain jobs cannot be identified with any precision. The wage paid men who are doing the same job in other establishments is not useful since it will ordinarily be found that a wide variety of rates are paid for this job within a community labor market. Comparable-worth advocates contend that a nondiscriminatory reference wage for female complainants is the wage paid men who are doing comparable work in the same establishment—work requiring equal levels of skill, effort, and responsibility. But that determination would be even more difficult than assessing the equality of work tasks for similar jobs have proven to be under the EPA.

The disparate-effects approach to discrimination also works better against job discrimination than wage discrimination. For example, facts can establish whether a firm's hiring practices exclude more women than men from employment and whether the difference is justified by business need. Whether female-dominated jobs have lower salaries than jobs held chiefly by males can also be factually established for more firms; however, the business justification for this outcome will almost always be the use of the labor market to establish the firm's wage rates, and that justification seems unchallengeable until Congress decides otherwise.

In view of these difficulties, I believe it would be wise to concentrate antidiscrimination efforts on equality of job access for women and other groups. Wage claims should be limited to acts of intentional discrimination that can be shown, for example, by sex differences in the methods of establishing wage rates (as in *Gunther*) and in the provision of health and pension benefits. This policy would eliminate little sex discrimination from the scope of enforcement efforts. Employers who want to discriminate against women are likely to do so by refusing to hire or promote them.

Wage discrimination is much more difficult to practice because, to hire and retain female employees, even a discriminatory employer must pay a competitive wage.

Implementation of this view would mean an acceptance, at least in public policy, of the structure of wages produced by the market and nongovernmental institutions, and it would concentrate effort on providing women with equal opportunity for all jobs. Some women will contend that this proposal is unsatisfactory because it would not increase the low wages paid for jobs that they prefer; many women do not want to become railroad engineers, for example, and therefore would not benefit from equal access to that job, even if it could be brought about. My response to this objection is that I am not willing to replace the market system of wage determination with a governmentally or judicially imposed system to change the nation's occupational wage structure. I do not contend that the wage structure produced by the market is completely fair. Far from it. But I prefer the market system of private decision making to one of public authority, and women themselves, through concerted action, can modify the market-produced structure of wages by means of collective bargaining and the efforts of occupational associations.

The women workers of this country are underpaid relative to men. The way to change that fact, I believe, is to offer women equal access to all jobs and to encourage private efforts to raise the relative wages of predominately female jobs. These methods would preserve a market-oriented system of wage determination based on the decisions of individuals and private parties, a system that our experience with the EPA demonstrates we should not give up.

NOTES

1. Equal Employment Opportunity Commission, *Annual Report* (1981), Washington, D.C., 1982, p. 9.

2. Ibid., p. 28.

INDEX

TABLE OF CASES

ABOUT THE AUTHOR

Walter Fogel has been Professor of Industrial Relations, University of California, Los Angeles, since 1962. He is also a labor arbitrator.

Professor Fogel has published many articles and books in the fields of labor economics and labor relations. His articles have appeared in *Industrial and Labor Relations Review, Journal of Human Resources*, and *Labor Law Journal*.

Professor Fogel holds a B.S. from North Dakota State University, an M.A. from the University of Minnesota, and a Ph.D. from the Massachusetts Institute of Technology.